The Book of
NATURAL DISASTERS

This edition produced in 1994 for **Shooting Star Press Inc**
230 Fifth Avenue, Suite 1212, New York, NY 10001

© Aladdin Books Ltd 1994

Designed and produced by
Aladdin Books Ltd, 28 Percy Street, London W1

Printed in the Czech Republic

ISBN 1-56924-069-8

Some of the material in this book was previously published in the Natural Disasters series.

The Book of
NATURAL DISASTERS

FOREWORD

Throughout the centuries people all over the world have lived in fear and wonder of natural disasters. Some strike without any warning leaving victims with no means of defense. Others can sometimes be predicted using increasingly sophisticated scientific equipment. With sufficient warning, it may be possible for people in the areas affected by natural disasters to protect themselves and their land by constructing artificial defenses or solutions. Dams, irrigation and famine aid, may minimize destruction, but it often becomes necessary for people to leave their homes in order to survive. The Book of Natural Disasters takes an exciting look at these dramatic events from famous disasters in history to the present day and their effects on the environment in the future.

Chapter One
VOLCANOES

CONTENTS

INTRODUCTION

A volcanic eruption is one of the most awesome and spectacular displays of nature's destructive power. In minutes, the fiery cloud of ash and rock that bursts from a mountain can transform a landscape. Even today, scientists cannot accurately predict the violence of volcanic eruptions, as was shown by the eruptions in June 1991 of Mt. Unzen in Japan and Mt. Pinatubo in the Philippines.

Yet for all their terrible power, volcanoes cannot be seen as purely destructive. The millions of tons of ash and lava that pour out have hardened into many of the earth's contours. In addition, the clouds of gases that are unleashed have helped to make up the atmosphere, and the steam produced has condensed to help to form the oceans.

WHAT IS A VOLCANO?

Volcanoes are openings in the surface of the earth, from which molten rock, called magma, and gases can escape.

The earth is made up of three layers – the crust, the mantle and the core. The crust is the outermost layer of rock and can be quite thin. The continental crust is between 20 and 30 miles thick, but the oceanic crust is only about 3 miles thick.

The crust feels solid but it consists of giant plates (see illustration, right) which float on the upper mantle. The upper mantle is made of hot, molten rock called magma which is always moving. Pressure in the mantle forces magma to the surface.

Volcanic eruptions occur where the rising magma finds a way through a crack or weakness in the earth's crust, usually at the edges of plates. These are called plate margins.

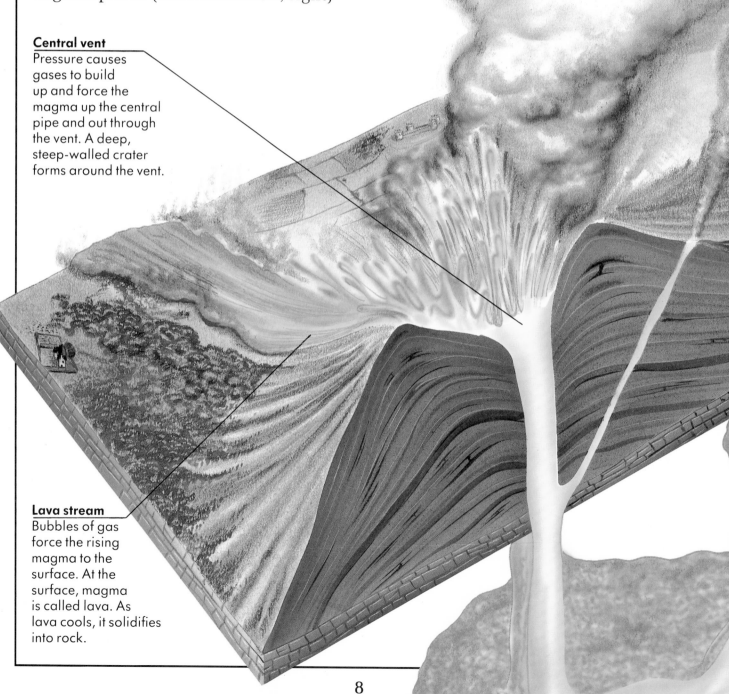

Central vent
Pressure causes gases to build up and force the magma up the central pipe and out through the vent. A deep, steep-walled crater forms around the vent.

Lava stream
Bubbles of gas force the rising magma to the surface. At the surface, magma is called lava. As lava cools, it solidifies into rock.

Layers

The steep slopes are built up of alternate layers of ash, and hardened lava. Sometimes lava bursts through in other places and forms other cones on the sides of the central cone.

Ash

The clouds of ash and gas that pour from the volcano help to form the cone shape around its vent. The ash consists of tiny pieces of lava, which harden into rock called tuff.

Magma

Magma collects in a chamber in the upper mantle. It is formed when two plates collide. The edge of one plate is dragged down under the other and melts into magma.

Plate movements

200 million years ago, all the land was joined together in one big continent called Pangaea. Gradually the pieces drifted apart and formed the seven continents we have today. Active volcanoes are usually found in definite zones, near plate margins. They are mostly caused by plate movement.

Active volcanoes marked in red

200 million years ago

100

50

Present day

Types of volcano

Thick, slow moving andesite lava builds up high, cone-shaped volcanoes. Andesite volcanoes are very violent.

Shield volcanoes form when runny lava escapes through a fissure and flows a long way. The volcano has broad sloping sides like a shield.

9

ACTIVE OR EXTINCT?

Active volcanoes are the ones that still erupt. They occur mainly at the edges of the earth's plates, where new crust is formed, and old crust is destroyed. Of the approximately 500 active volcanoes in the world, 20-30 erupt each year, such as Nevado del Ruiz in Colombia, South America.

Dormant, or "sleeping," volcanoes are those that are quiet for a long time and then suddenly erupt again. Two examples are Mount Fujiyama in Japan, which last erupted in 1707, and Mount Rainier in Washington, which has not erupted for over 100 years. Both these volcanoes still have lava bubbling in the crater and steam rising from them. No one knows when they may erupt again.

An extinct volcano is one that has not erupted for thousands of years. Mount Egremont in New Zealand and Mount Kilimanjaro in Tanzania, Africa, are examples of extinct volcanoes. But even "extinct" volcanoes can suddenly erupt, as Tristan da Cunha and Helgafell in Iceland showed!

▲ **Mount Fujiyama in Hondo, Japan, has been dormant since 1707.**

▶ **Edinburgh Castle, Scotland, is built on the remains of a volcano, extinct for 325 million years.**

▶ **(Main picture) The eruption of Mauna Loa, on Hawaii. At 13,684 ft high, it is the world's largest active volcano. Hawaii is the only island in the chain of Hawaiian islands which still has active volcanoes.**

The volcanoes that erupted again

Tristan da Cunha (below) is a volcanic island in the South Atlantic Ocean which was believed to be extinct. In 1961, it suddenly erupted again. The 270 islanders escaped in boats.

In 1973, the "extinct" volcano of Helgafell erupted on the Icelandic island of Heimaey. The people escaped, but many houses were buried or burned by the red-hot lava flows that flowed towards the island's fishing port.

WHEN A VOLCANO ERUPTS

Volcanoes are in a sense the safety valves in the earth's crust, releasing the buildup of pressure caused by gases beneath the earth's surface.

The strength of a volcanic eruption depends on the type of magma and the amount of gases trapped in it. The magma formed when plates pull apart is very fluid. The gases in it have time to escape and there is no violent eruption. When plates collide, however, the magma formed is much thicker and stickier. Gases become trapped in it and escape explosively in a huge cloud of steam and dust thousands of feet high.

A volcano may be quiet for many years before it erupts again. Often its slopes are covered with grass and trees, like an ordinary mountain. A thin wisp of vapor rising from the crater may be the only sign that it is a still-active volcano.

Surges of red-hot lava flood out of the volcano's crater at speeds of up to 600 ft per second. Lava will flow from the volcano as long as there is enough pressure to force it to the surface. After such violent eruptions, the entire volcano often collapses into its empty magma chamber, forming a steep-sided depression. This is called a caldera.

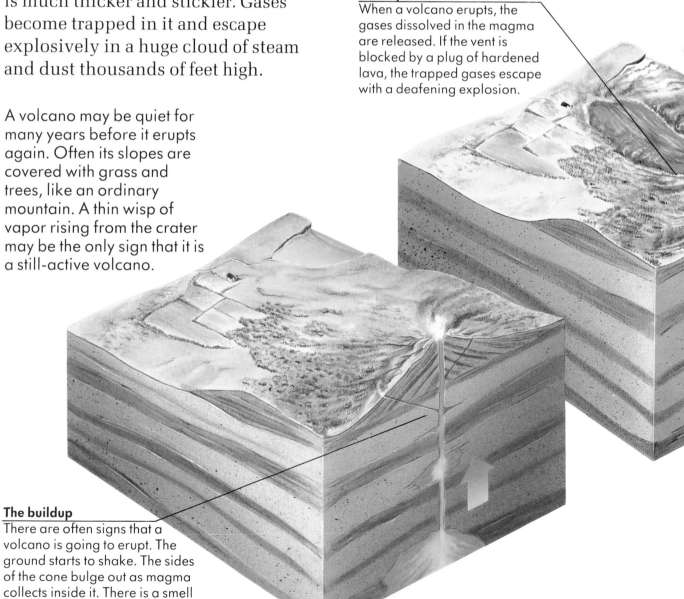

The explosion
When a volcano erupts, the gases dissolved in the magma are released. If the vent is blocked by a plug of hardened lava, the trapped gases escape with a deafening explosion.

The buildup
There are often signs that a volcano is going to erupt. The ground starts to shake. The sides of the cone bulge out as magma collects inside it. There is a smell of sulfur as gases escape through cracks in the rocks.

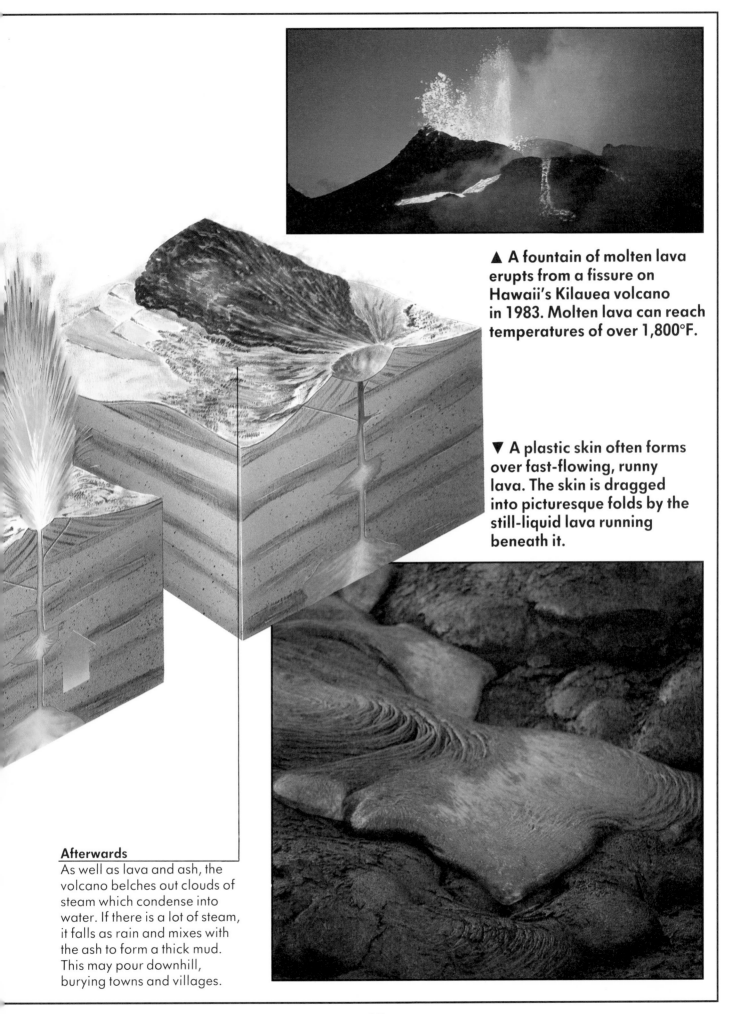

▲ A fountain of molten lava erupts from a fissure on Hawaii's Kilauea volcano in 1983. Molten lava can reach temperatures of over 1,800°F.

▼ A plastic skin often forms over fast-flowing, runny lava. The skin is dragged into picturesque folds by the still-liquid lava running beneath it.

Afterwards

As well as lava and ash, the volcano belches out clouds of steam which condense into water. If there is a lot of steam, it falls as rain and mixes with the ash to form a thick mud. This may pour downhill, burying towns and villages.

VOLCANOES UNDER THE SEA

The largest number of volcanoes is found under the seafloor. The ocean floor is very thin and it can be easily pierced by the magma which lies underneath, especially along the lines of weakness at plate margins. One such plate margin runs down the Atlantic Ocean. When the plates move apart, rising magma seeps up into the gap and hardens into a new strip of crust. This makes the Atlantic wider, and so forces Europe and North America further apart.

The earth is not getting bigger so, if new crust forms in one place, old crust must disappear in another. More than half the world's volcanoes occur in a belt around the Pacific Ocean, known as the Ring of Fire. They form when plates collide and old crust has been dragged back into the mantle.

Sometimes volcanoes form when a crustal plate moves over a "hot spot" in the earth's mantle. Molten magma bores upwards from a fixed positon deep below the ocean floor and breaks through the drifting plates to form shield volcanoes, like the Hawaiian islands.

The finished island
After many eruptions, the mountain breaks through the surface like the tip of an iceberg.

The beginning
Most of the volcanoes under the sea are totally submerged. The first hint of activity can often be picked up by seismographs, which detect movements in the earth as the magma builds up.

The eruption
Near the surface, undersea volcanoes usually erupt violently. The hot molten lava explodes when it hits the cold sea water, spewing out thick, black clouds of steam and ash.

▼ Birds also help to carry seed to the new island.

New life
At first the newly-created island is bare rock. Soil is formed from tiny bits of volcanic rock worn away by wind and water. Seeds are carried there by the wind, and take root. Soon plants, like the cacti below, and insects flourish there.

▼ This picture shows recent lava formations found on the crest of the East Pacific rise.

VOLCANOES IN HISTORY

Today, the spectacular displays of energy produced by volcanoes provide clues to the earth's evolution and the nature of its interior. But for thousands of years, people did not understand why a mountain suddenly burst apart and fiery liquid poured out. The effects of volcanoes were even more devastating than they are today, because people could not recognize the warning signs.

One of the most famous volcanic disasters was in AD 79, when Mount Vesuvius in southern Italy erupted. The volcano had been quiet for centuries. People farmed the land on the cone, and two important towns, Pompeii and Herculaneum, had grown up near its foot. There had been earthquakes but they were not seen as a sign that the volcano might erupt. One day, seemingly without warning, a massive explosion blew off the top of Vesuvius. The town of Pompeii was buried in ash and more than 20,000 inhabitants were killed.

Pompeii

The thunderous eruption of Vesuvius left the surrounding countryside unrecognizable. Pompeii was buried under 20 ft of ash, and steam and mud combined to form the torrent that engulfed Herculaneum in 50 ft of volcanic mud.

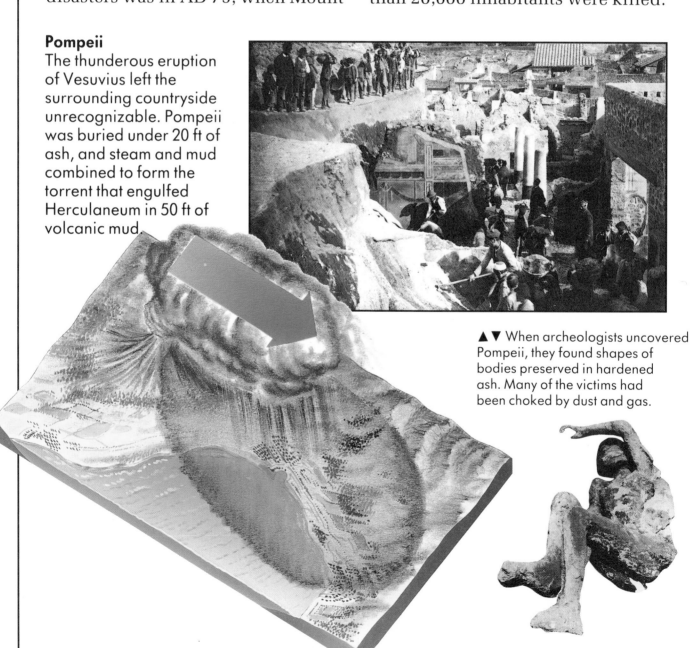

▲ ▼ When archeologists uncovered Pompeii, they found shapes of bodies preserved in hardened ash. Many of the victims had been choked by dust and gas.

Volcanoes in legend

The legend of Atlantis tells of a mighty island empire, described by the Greek philosopher Plato in 360 BC, which mysteriously disappeared into the sea.

Recent evidence suggests that Atlantis was on the Greek island of Thera, now known as Santorini, and that it was devastated in 1470 BC by one of the most powerful volcanic eruptions ever recorded. There were no survivors. When the volcano stopped erupting, its empty shell collapsed into a 590 ft-deep crater in the sea, causing a massive tidal wave which destroyed most of near by Crete.

▲ Many volcanoes today are tourist attractions, such as the remains of Vesuvius (above).

◄ Mount Etna is situated on the island of Sicily. It is Europe's highest, most continuously active volcano. Etna has erupted at least 400 times in the last 2,500 years.

KRAKATAU ERUPTS

The loudest and most violent explosion in modern times was in 1883 when the uninhabited Indonesian island of Krakatau erupted and was almost completely destroyed. Krakatau was the stump of an old volcano, but had not erupted for 200 years, and the central vent was blocked by a plug of solid lava. However, pressure was building up under the plug. Krakatau was getting ready to blow its top.

At 10:02 a.m. on August 27, the whole mountain erupted, ripping the island apart. The explosion was so loud it was heard in Australia, over 3,000 mi away. Rocks were thrown more than 30 mi into the air. A massive cloud of ash darkened the skies for almost 300 mi around.

The eruption caused a 115 foot high tidal wave, or tsunami, which destroyed 163 villages on nearby islands. More than 36,000 people were drowned.

THE ERUPTION OF KRAKATAU

MALAYSIA

Singapore •

SUMATRA

BORNEO

Krakatau   JAVA

The first signs
A series of small explosions occurred as gases began to escape. The volcano's walls collapsed, and steam built up as sea water poured onto the hot magma below.

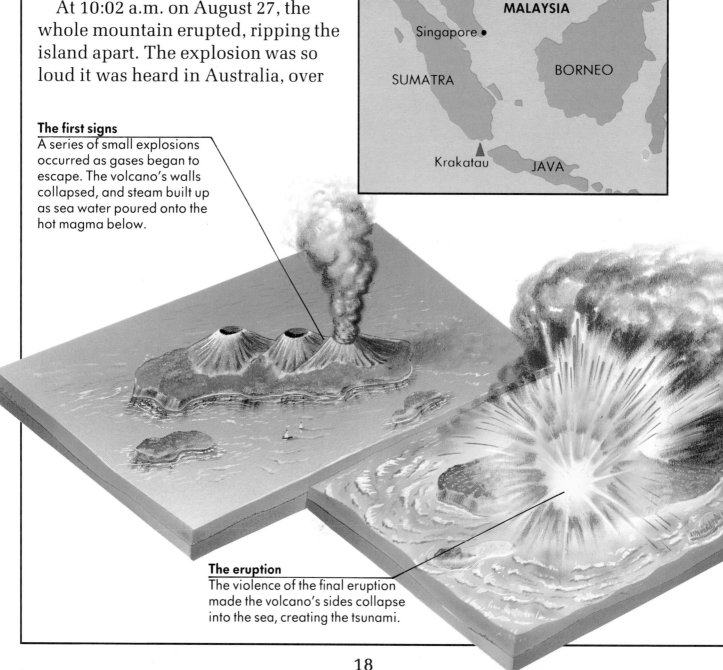

The eruption
The violence of the final eruption made the volcano's sides collapse into the sea, creating the tsunami.

▲ An illustration of a steamer in Sumatra, beached by the tidal wave from the eruption of nearby Krakatau.
▼ Anak Krakatau. Evidence of recent lava flows can be seen here.

After the blast
The volcano was still active, and by 1927, a new island had been created called Anak Krakatau (Child of Krakatau).

NEW VOLCANOES

In 1943, a farmer from the village of Paricutín in Mexico noticed that a crack in his cornfield was getting longer. In February that year, the ground began to shake. Steam and gases poured out, and lava shot up into the air. By the end of the week, the cone was 500 feet high. In 1944, when the volcano was 1,230 feet high, fiery lava flows destroyed a nearby town. The volcano continued to be active until 1952, by which time it was 9,090 feet high.

Volcanic eruptions occur more frequently underwater than on land. In 1963, some fishermen saw clouds of smoke rising from the sea near Iceland. It was coming from a volcano on the sea bed. Soon steam and lava were being flung into the air. A day later, a small island had appeared above the surface. By the time the eruptions stopped, the highest point was over 435 feet high. The new island was named Surtsey, after the Icelandic god of fire.

▶▲ Surtsey erupted for several months. It gave scientists a rare chance to watch a new island grow. When the eruptions stopped, the island covered 1 square mile.

▶ Scientists could also study the development of life on the island. Plants began to grow again only a few months after it had formed.

(Main picture) A cloud of steam and ash rises from the newborn island of Surtsey. For three years, Surtsey provided spectacular evidence of volcanic activity along the plate margins in the Atlantic Ocean.

CHANGING THE LANDSCAPE

One of the simplest ways volcanoes change the landscape is by forming new rock. Rock formed from hardened magma or lava is called igneous rock from the Latin word *ignis*, meaning fire. The dark, runny lava that flows out of fissures hardens into an igneous rock called basalt. The lava from andesite volcanoes is lighter in color because it contains large amounts of the mineral silica. If gas is trapped in the lava, it hardens into pumice, which is a very light rock filled with gas bubbles. Granite is a rough, grainy kind of igneous rock formed when magma cools in the crust.

▲ Layers of volcanic ash near Caldeira das Sete Cidades in the Azores.

▼ Pahoehoe, or ropy lava, has a smooth, twisted surface.

▼ Volcanic needles spike into the skyline on Tenerife.

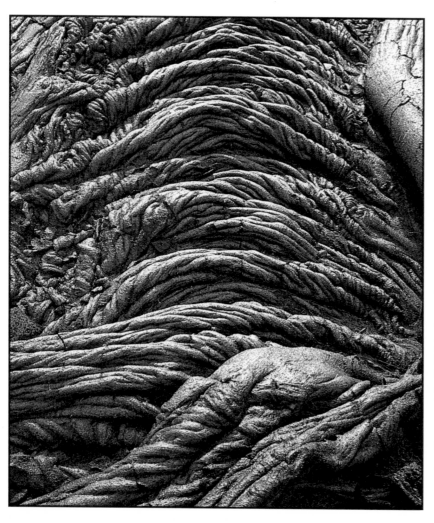

Mount Erebus

Mount Erebus is the only active volcano in Antarctica. It consists of three older craters, in addition to the current active one. The tip is covered with snow, but lava bubbles in the main crater. Steam that pours out from fumaroles, or openings in the ground, has frozen around the volcano's vent to form ice chimneys, which are over 65 feet in height.

Although there are no active volcanoes in Britain or France, ancient eruptions have left their mark on the landscape. Edinburgh Castle in Scotland and the chapel at Le Puy in France are both built on volcanic plugs of lava. The Giant's Causeway in Northern Ireland looks like huge stepping stones. The rocks are basalt formed from cooled basalt lava.

Crater Lake sits on top of an extinct volcano in Oregon. Despite its name, it is not a crater. When magma stops rising in a volcano, the top of the mountain may collapse into the empty magma chamber below, forming a deep, hollow caldera. Calderas are often filled by a lake. Crater Lake is 2,000 feet deep and six miles wide. The empty caldera of Ngorongoro Crater in Tanzania, Africa, is now a wildlife reserve.

DO VOLCANOES AFFECT US?

Many people near volcanoes live in the fear of an eruption, which would force them to flee their homes. But can volcanoes affect us all?

When volcanoes erupt they emit gases, including carbon dioxide and sulfur dioxide. Carbon dioxide is a greenhouse gas. This means that it helps to keep the earth warm. In the past, the amount of carbon dioxide released by volcanoes helped to maintain the balance of gases in the atmosphere. However, this balance is now being upset. Burning fossil fuels and cutting down and burning trees both produce large amounts of carbon dioxide. If too much carbon dioxide is trapped, temperatures around the world could go up.

The sulfur dioxide produced by volcanoes contributes to the problem of acid rain. When it mixes with water vapor in the air, it forms a very weak acid. This acid then falls to the ground in rain, snow, or dust.

Industry
Factories and power plants burn coal, oil, or gas and belch out smoke which contains carbon dioxide. Industry is a major cause of air pollution.

Domestic/traffic
Home heating systems and motor vehicles burn fuels, producing carbon dioxide.

Destroying forests
Plants absorb carbon dioxide and release the oxygen we breathe. Huge areas of forest have been destroyed.

Transport
The nitrogen oxides in the exhaust fumes of airplanes add to pollution in the air.

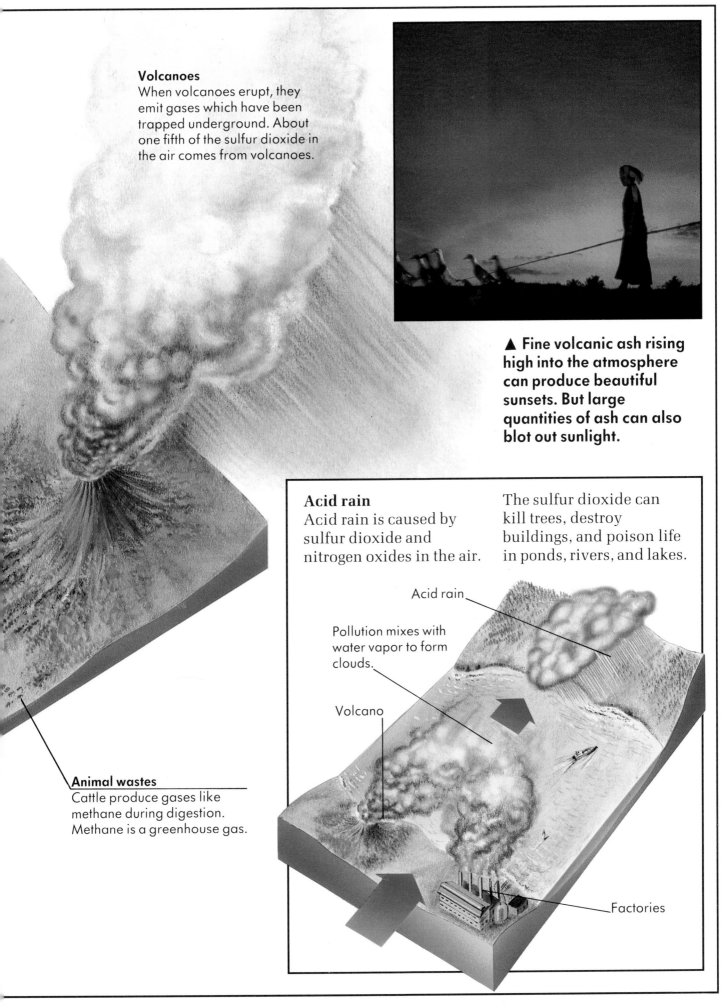

Volcanoes

When volcanoes erupt, they emit gases which have been trapped underground. About one fifth of the sulfur dioxide in the air comes from volcanoes.

▲ **Fine volcanic ash rising high into the atmosphere can produce beautiful sunsets. But large quantities of ash can also blot out sunlight.**

Animal wastes

Cattle produce gases like methane during digestion. Methane is a greenhouse gas.

Acid rain

Acid rain is caused by sulfur dioxide and nitrogen oxides in the air. The sulfur dioxide can kill trees, destroy buildings, and poison life in ponds, rivers, and lakes.

Acid rain

Pollution mixes with water vapor to form clouds.

Volcano

Factories

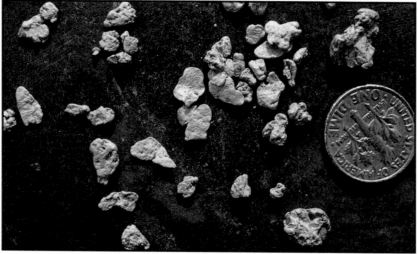

▲ This farm in Lanzarote is situated in the crater of an extinct volcano where the fertile soil provides ideal growing conditions.

◄ The heat from volcanoes makes metals in the crust melt and flow through cracks in the rocks, where they cool and solidify. Gold, shown left, is often mined from the remains of old volcanoes.

ARE VOLCANOES ALL BAD?

An active volcano can erupt at any time. Yet many farms and villages are built on the slopes of volcanoes. So why do people take such risks?

One reason is that the soil is very fertile. In India the ancient basalt lava flows from volcanic eruptions in the past have eroded into the rich black soil of the Deccan Plateau, where cotton is now grown. Farmers in Indonesia grow rice in volcanic soil, and there are vineyards and orange and lemon groves on the slopes of Mount Etna.

Geothermal energy, or energy from the earth is another vital resource of volcanic areas. It would take 20,000 times the world's coal supply to produce the heat that exists in the upper 7 miles of the earth's crust. Today, many geothermal power plants have been built in Iceland, New Zealand, and Japan, where groundwater and magma provide hot water and steam. As supplies of fossil fuels run out, geothermal energy is a relatively clean and almost endless energy resource for the future.

Alternative energy

Water seeps through layers of porous rock, like limestone, until it meets a layer of impermeable rock such as granite. The water collects in the tiny spaces between the grains of the rock, and is heated by the hot rocks of the volcano to produce steam. This steam is piped to power plants where it is used to turn the turbines of an electricity generator. Geothermal energy can also provide heat for other sources, such as these greenhouses in Iceland, shown below.

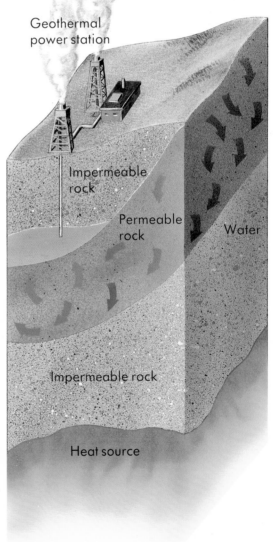

Geothermal power station

Impermeable rock

Permeable rock

Water

Impermeable rock

Heat source

WHAT CAN WE DO?

We cannot stop volcanoes from erupting and we cannot prevent people from living near them and taking advantage of the fertile soil to grow their crops. So can we prevent future disasters where people are killed and towns destroyed?

Scientists try to give warnings about future eruptions so that people can be evacuated. They study movements in the rocks beneath the earth's surface. Rising magma creates a series of tiny earthquakes which can be used as early warnings. The volcano's shape can also be monitored. As the magma chamber fills up, it begins to swell or bulge, which indicates that the volcano is on the verge of erupting.

However, to a large extent, volcanoes remain a mystery to science. Predicting eruptions is still an uncertain and dangerous business, as was proven by the recent deaths of two leading vulcanologists, Maurice and Katia Krafft, at Mt. Unzen in Japan in June, 1991.

◄ Laser beams, shown here on Mount Pelee, in Martinique, are used to predict volcanic eruptions. A swelling on the volcano caused by the buildup of magma can be detected by a change in the length of the laser beam.

◄◄ Using a canvas glove to protect his hand from the heat, this vulcanologist takes a sample of molten rock with a geological pick. By analyzing samples, scientists can estimate the source of the molten rock.

▲ When Mt. Etna erupted in 1983, dynamite was used in an attempt to control the flow of lava. The aim of the operation was to divert the flow of lava into an inactive crater on the volcano. The men shown above are building a canal which will carry the lava to the desired crater. The dynamite is placed in a specially-designed wall, which can be seen in the picture, and later blown up to create a "path" between the lava flow and the canal, which leads to the crater.

FACTFILE: *Volcanoes*

The greatest eruption

In 1815, Tambora, an Indonesian volcano, erupted, leaving a caldera 4 mi across. 4.5 cubic miles of rock were flung out. This is far more than Krakatau ejected, even though Krakatau was louder. The largest caldera on earth is Lake Toba in Sumatra, Indonesia. It is 31 mi long and 13 mi wide.

The Hawaiian islands

The plate which contains the Hawaiian islands is slowly drifting over the hot spot which formed the volcanoes. Midway island, at the western end of the chain, was the first to form. It is 27 million years old. Hawaii itself is at the eastern end and is the youngest island. It is 700,000 years old.

The greatest loss of life

The largest loss of life from a volcano happened in 1902 when Mount Pelée, on the Caribbean island of Martinique, erupted. A glowing hot cloud of lava, gases, and ash poured down the mountain onto the town of St. Pierre in the valley below. About 30,000 people in the town died. They had no time to escape as the avalanche raced towards them at over 125 miles an hour.

The highest active volcanoes

Antofalla, Argentina (21,160 ft)
Guallatiri, Chile (19,882 ft)
Cotopaxi, Ecuador (19,347 ft)
Sangay, Ecuador (17,159 ft)
Klyuchevskaya, Soviet Union (15,584 ft)
Wrangell, Alaska (14,163 ft)
Mauna Loa, Hawaii (13,684 ft)
Galeras, Ecuador (13,684 ft)
Cameroun, Cameroon (13,353 ft)

Recent volcanoes

On June 3, 1991, Mount Unzen in Japan exploded, sending lava cascading down the mountainside at 100 mph. Thirty-eight people were killed. Geologists were ready for the eruption. The volcano had killed 15,000 people in 1792 and there were signs that it might erupt again. The area was evacuated, but the advance warning brought people to watch the volcano erupt. Among those killed were geologists studying the eruption and journalists reporting on it.

Only a few days later, on June 12, Mount Pinatubo in the Philippines erupted with an explosion that sounded like an atomic bomb. A mushroom of smoke billowed more than 85,300 feet into the air (see left), masking the sun. Pinatubo had been dormant for 600 years. There was no advance warning of this eruption. However, there was enough time to evacuate 30,000 people, mainly tribesmen from hillside villages and American troops at a nearby air base. Two people were killed by the initial explosion, a small boy who breathed in volcanic fumes and a man whose car crashed when the cloud of smoke and ash blotted out the sun. However, recent ash falls from the volcano have smothered the landscape, buildings and cars have been crushed, and the death toll is thought to be over 200.

Chapter Two
EARTHQUAKES

CONTENTS

INTRODUCTION

The destructive power of an earthquake is one of the most violent and deadly of all natural forces. In just a few seconds, these massive vibrations of the earth's crust can shatter whole communities. The earthquakes that are unleashed on some of the world's most densely populated areas are not necessarily the largest. Yet they cause the greatest amount of damage and the highest number of deaths. Scientists hope to avoid such devastating losses by developing more accurate methods of earthquake prediction.

WHAT IS AN EARTHQUAKE?

An earthquake is the sudden, and often violent, trembling of part of the earth's surface. It sends shock waves racing through the earth's crust, which is the name given to the rocky outer layer surrounding the earth. Earthquakes are generated in the huge tilelike sections, called plates, which make up this crust.

A plate boundary is the area where two of these plates meet. Continual movement at plate boundaries creates a buildup of pressure beneath the surface. Rocks are elastic up to a point and can absorb the strain from this pressure for hundreds, even thousands, of years. Eventually, however, they snap, or rupture, at their weakest point, relieving the enormous strain. Huge amounts of energy are released as shock waves, called seismic waves, radiate outward from the point where the rocks fractured. The area within the earth's crust where the shock waves begin is called the earthquake's focus. The place on the surface directly above the focus is the epicenter.

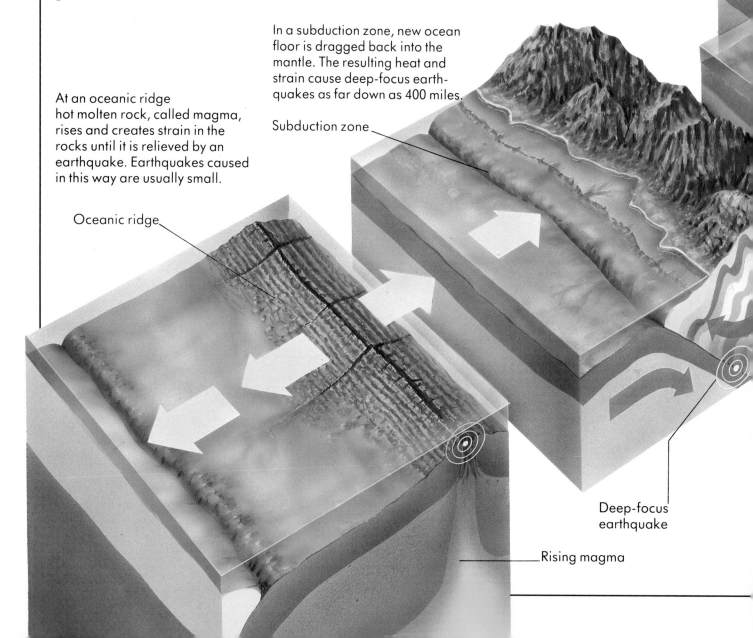

In a subduction zone, new ocean floor is dragged back into the mantle. The resulting heat and strain cause deep-focus earthquakes as far down as 400 miles.

Subduction zone

At an oceanic ridge hot molten rock, called magma, rises and creates strain in the rocks until it is relieved by an earthquake. Earthquakes caused in this way are usually small.

Oceanic ridge

Deep-focus earthquake

Rising magma

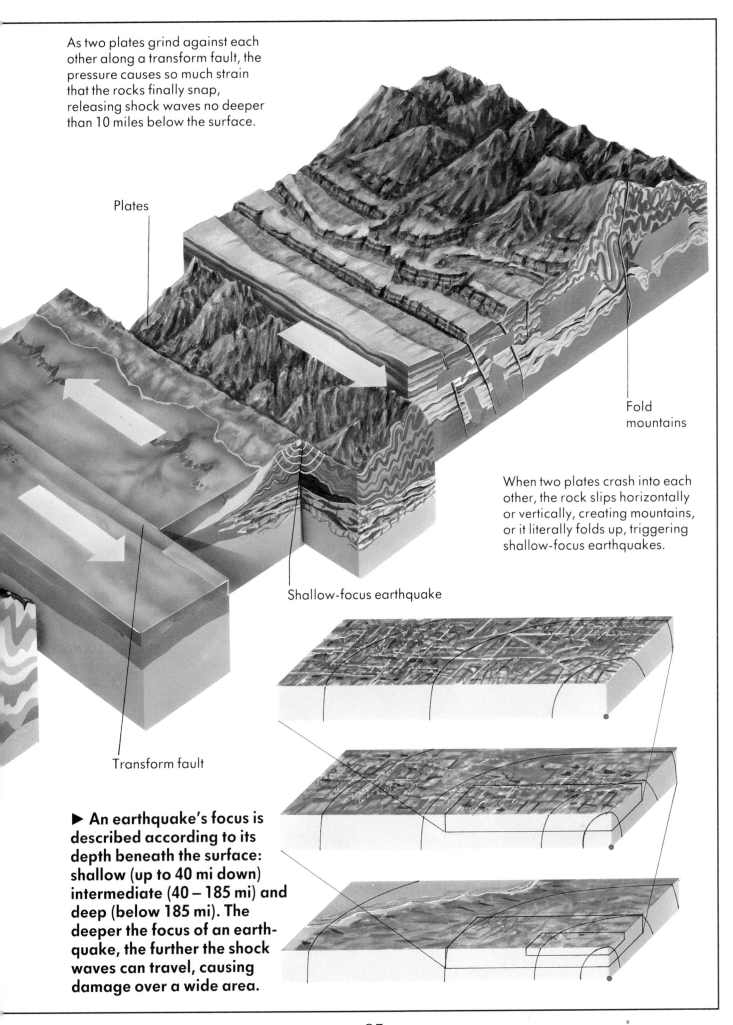

As two plates grind against each other along a transform fault, the pressure causes so much strain that the rocks finally snap, releasing shock waves no deeper than 10 miles below the surface.

Plates

Fold mountains

When two plates crash into each other, the rock slips horizontally or vertically, creating mountains, or it literally folds up, triggering shallow-focus earthquakes.

Shallow-focus earthquake

Transform fault

▶ **An earthquake's focus is described according to its depth beneath the surface: shallow (up to 40 mi down) intermediate (40 – 185 mi) and deep (below 185 mi). The deeper the focus of an earthquake, the further the shock waves can travel, causing damage over a wide area.**

THE MOVING EARTH

The earth consists of three separate layers: the crust, the mantle, and the core. The crust is made of giant plates which are constantly moving. The plates float in the hot molten rock, called magma, of the upper mantle. Pressure in the mantle forces the magma up through the crust along the oceanic ridges. These areas are known as constructive plate margins because when the magma cools and hardens, it forms new ocean floor.

In subduction zones, or destructive plate margins, ocean floor is destroyed when plates collide and the edge of one plate is dragged down into the mantle. At a third type of boundary, the transform fault, plates are simply sliding past each other, and so the fault is neither a constructive nor a destructive boundary. Plate movements at all three types of boundary can give rise to earthquakes.

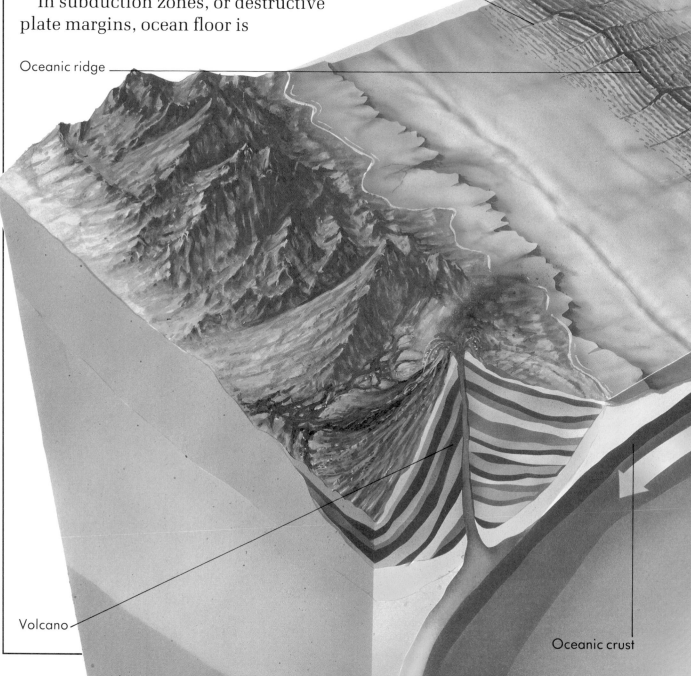

Transform fault

Oceanic ridge

Volcano

Oceanic crust

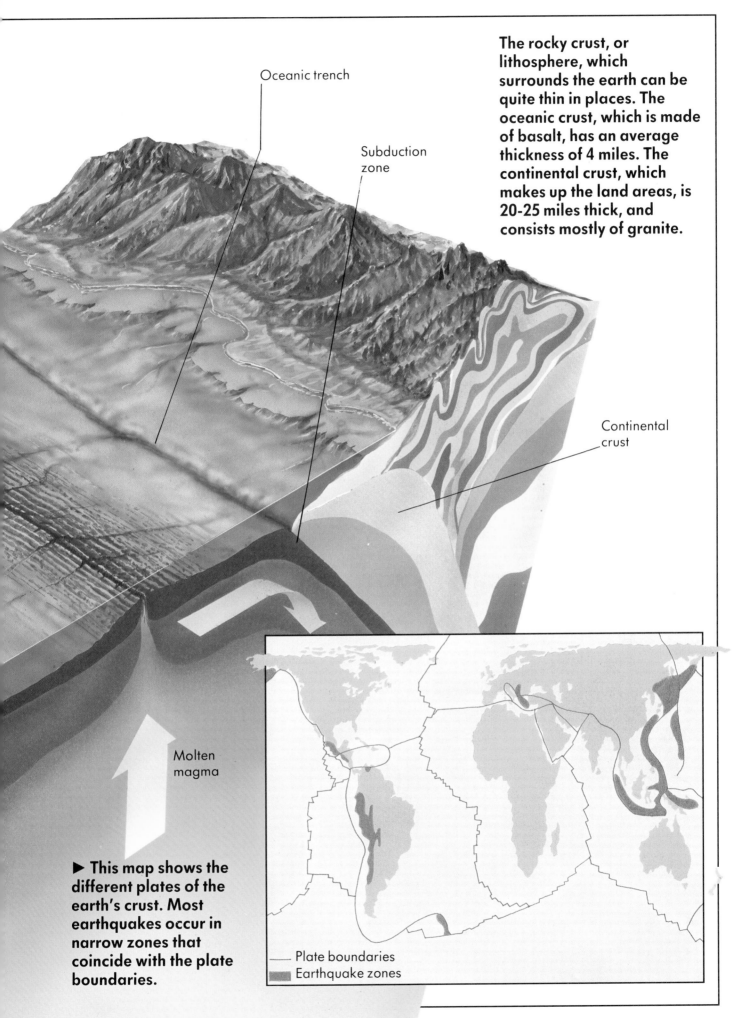

Oceanic trench

Subduction zone

The rocky crust, or lithosphere, which surrounds the earth can be quite thin in places. The oceanic crust, which is made of basalt, has an average thickness of 4 miles. The continental crust, which makes up the land areas, is 20-25 miles thick, and consists mostly of granite.

Continental crust

Molten magma

▶ This map shows the different plates of the earth's crust. Most earthquakes occur in narrow zones that coincide with the plate boundaries.

— Plate boundaries
▨ Earthquake zones

AN EARTHQUAKE BEGINS

In the period before an earthquake, the pressure building up in the rock layers beneath the ground causes so much strain that cracks appear in walls and pavements. When the rocks finally snap, the first seismic waves to be released from the earthquake's focus are known as body waves. Body waves travel through the earth and are of two types: primary (P) and secondary (S) waves. Waves that only travel along the surface of the earth are surface, or long (L), waves.

Primary waves travel through solid rock, volcanic lava, water and even air at speeds of up to 5 miles per second. P waves are followed by S waves, which travel more slowly at about 3¾ miles per second. When the body waves reach the surface, some are transformed into surface waves. Surface waves produce the most severe ground movements. A violent jolt is felt at the epicenter as the ground moves. The first tremor may last for only 30-60 seconds, but further tremors, or aftershocks, occur soon after as the disturbed rocks settle into a new position.

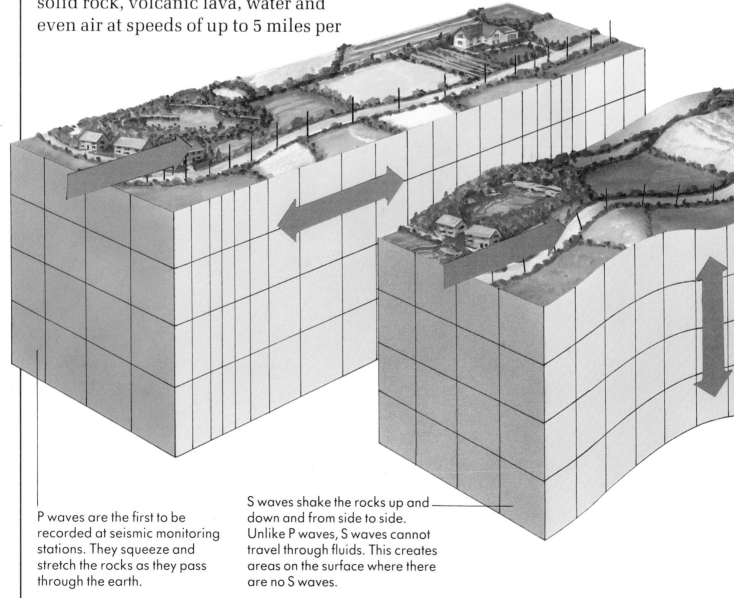

P waves are the first to be recorded at seismic monitoring stations. They squeeze and stretch the rocks as they pass through the earth.

S waves shake the rocks up and down and from side to side. Unlike P waves, S waves cannot travel through fluids. This creates areas on the surface where there are no S waves.

Telltale signs

Certain warning signs have been noticed before an earthquake. Minor tremors make the ground shake gently. As the rocks beneath begin to warp and bulge, swellings appear on the surface. They cause the ground to crack and finally burst open (shown right). Scientists in China have noticed that water in ponds and canals gives off strange smells, possibly due to the buildup of gas underground.

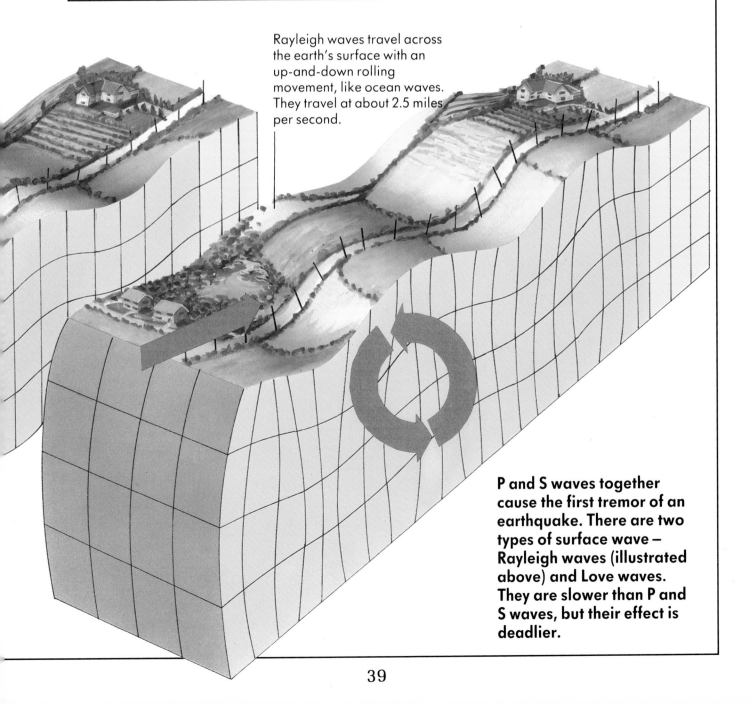

Rayleigh waves travel across the earth's surface with an up-and-down rolling movement, like ocean waves. They travel at about 2.5 miles per second.

P and S waves together cause the first tremor of an earthquake. There are two types of surface wave – Rayleigh waves (illustrated above) and Love waves. They are slower than P and S waves, but their effect is deadlier.

DEATH AND DESTRUCTION

As the roar and violent motion of a major earthquake are heard and felt, tall apartment buildings and office blocks often collapse in vast piles of rubble, burying hundreds of people. In Mexico City in 1985, the main tower of the Benito Juárez Hospital collapsed floor by floor, killing 1,000 patients and staff. Huge cracks appear as roads and pavements are ripped apart, and road and rail links to the stricken area are often cut off, making it difficult for rescue workers to bring help. There is also a serious risk of fire from damaged electricity cables and gas pipes.

Earthquakes bring with them other deadly aftereffects. Those that occur under the sea create giant waves, called *tsunamis*, which sweep in from the sea and lash the coast. The 1964 Alaskan quake created a *tsunami*, 70 ft high in places, which raced toward Hawaii at over 400 mph. Strong tremors cause nearby rivers to overflow, and dams and reservoirs to burst, triggering off huge landslides. An earthquake in Peru in 1971 caused a massive chunk of ice to break off Mt Huascarán in the Andes Mountains. As the ice melted, it turned into a 260 ft-high mudflow which swept through the town of Yungay, killing 50,000 people.

Before and after

Mexico City (below), is built on layers of mud, clay, gravel and sand of a dried-up lake bed. Soil levels and buildings there can subside by up to 6 inches a year. Cities built on soft surfaces suffer most earthquake damage because the soft soil increases the effects of the seismic waves.

Amazingly, the 52-story headquarters of Mexico's state oil company, the tallest tower in Latin America, survived the shock waves of the 1985 earthquake. With the aid of special equipment, several dozen babies were rescued alive from the ruins of the city's hospitals.

► After the 1989 earthquake in San Francisco (63 dead and almost 4,000 injured), losses across the city totalled $6 billion.

▼ The earthquake in the Indian state of Uttar Pradesh on October 20, 1991 caused widespread structural damage to bridges and roads.

MEASURING EARTHQUAKES

The scientists who study the seismic waves released from the focus of an earthquake are called seismologists. Special measuring instruments, called seismographs, record the pattern of the seismic waves. Seismologists use these patterns to determine the strength and duration of an earthquake, as well as the amount of movement along a fault line. Taking readings at several different points on the earth's surface also helps them to pinpoint the exact location of the earthquake's focus.

Two different scales are used to measure the strength of an earthquake. The most common one is the Richter scale, devised by American seismologist, Charles Richter, in 1935. It calculates the magnitude of an earthquake from seismograph recordings that measure the amount of energy released. An increase of 1 point on the Richter scale means that an earthquake is 10 times stronger than one with the next value below. An earthquake measuring less than 5 on the Richter scale causes minimal damage, while a major earthquake measures 7 or more. The second scale is the Mercalli scale, which calculates the intensity of an earthquake by assessing the damage it causes.

I: Felt by only a very few people. II: Felt by a few, on upper floors.

III: Similar to a passing vehicle.
IV: Felt by many people indoors.

V: Buildings tremble and trees shake.
VI: Felt by all. Plaster cracks.

VII: Bricks loosen. Difficult to stand. VIII: Damage to weak structures.

Jagged tracings (right) are made as the seismograph records the movements of the ground during an earthquake. Scientists can distinguish between the primary, secondary, and surface waves.

IX: Pipes crack. Buildings collapse. X: Huge ground cracks. Landslides.

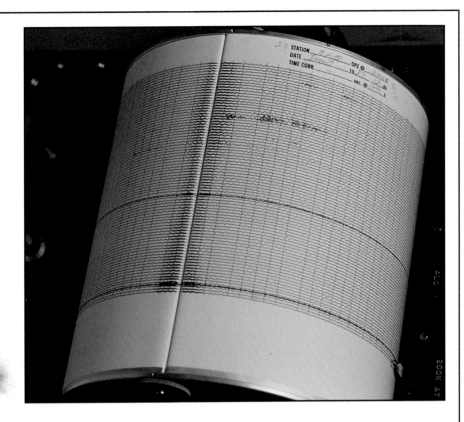

◄ **The Mercalli scale was invented in 1902 by Italian seismologist, Giuseppe Mercalli, and modified during the 1930s by American scientists. The scale describes effects that range from tiny swaying movements (I) to total devastation (XII).**

XI: Most buildings destroyed. *Tsunamis*. XII: Total destruction. Surface waves seen.

Seismographs

One type of seismograph records the horizontal movements of the earth, and the other type vertical movements. A weight is attached to a frame by a sensitive spring. As the ground trembles, the weight remains stationary but the frame moves and a pen records the movement on paper wrapped around a rotating drum. This recording is called a seismogram.

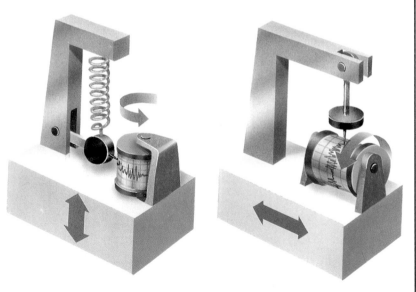

43

EARTHQUAKES IN HISTORY

Many of the myths and legends surrounding earthquakes date back thousands of years. Some of the world's greatest civilizations have been built up around major earthquake zones such as China, the mountainous areas of the Middle East, Mexico, and the lands around the Mediterranean Sea and India.

Primitive peoples believed that earthquakes were caused by the actions of huge beasts. Hindu mythology claimed that the earth was supported by eight huge elephants. When one of the elephants became tired and lowered and shook its head, this resulted in an earthquake. According to Japanese legend, earthquakes are caused by the *namazu*, a giant catfish living in the mud beneath the earth's surface. The *namazu* is something of a prankster who can only be controlled by the Kashima god. In October 1855, when the gods were said to be visiting a distant shrine, an earthquake struck the city of Edo (modern Tokyo). In the absence of the Kashima god, the catfish had hurled itself around and unleashed the earthquake.

▼ The Japanese legend of the *namazu* was depicted in many popular 19th-century prints. The one below shows the people of Edo attacking the *namazu* for unleashing the earthquake.

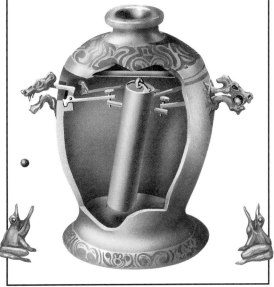

The first earthquake sensor
This instrument was designed by the Chinese in the 2nd century A.D. During a tremor, a swinging weight opened the mouth of one of eight dragons. A small bronze ball dropped from the dragon's mouth onto the open-mouthed frog below, making a loud clang. The dragon with the empty mouth indicated the direction of the earthquake.

▲ The earthquake that devastated the Jamaican city of Port Royal (above) in 1692 left 2,000 people dead. Port Royal was an important pirate center for the West Indies, trading in slaves and rum. Many people believed that the earthquake was a punishment from God.

► This engraving shows one of the effects of the earthquake that struck the Calabria region of southern Italy in 1783. About 50,000 people died in a series of earthquakes over a 7-week period. Later, the Academy of Sciences and Fine Letters in Naples set up a commission to assess the damage.

THE SAN ANDREAS FAULT

The giant San Andreas fault system stretches for more than 750 miles along the coast of California. This transform fault lies along the boundary between the Pacific Plate and the North American Plate. As these two plates constantly grind against each other, some of the resulting strain is released from time to time by tiny quakes. But when the plates become locked together, this prevents any release. The pressure builds up over a period of years until a massive quake occurs, such as the one on April 18, 1906. Although the earthquake only lasted for 40 seconds, its force (Richter scale 8.3) was enormous. In San Francisco, 700 people died, over 28,000 buildings were ruined, and over 250,000 people were left homeless.

Today, evidence of the San Andreas fault can be seen in cracked walls and and scared landscapes below.

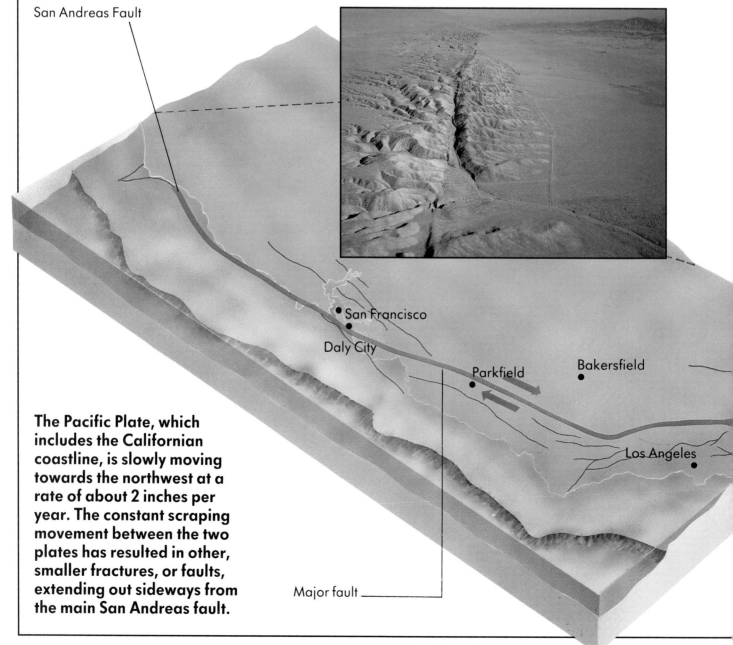

San Andreas Fault

San Francisco

Daly City

Parkfield

Bakersfield

Los Angeles

The Pacific Plate, which includes the Californian coastline, is slowly moving towards the northwest at a rate of about 2 inches per year. The constant scraping movement between the two plates has resulted in other, smaller fractures, or faults, extending out sideways from the main San Andreas fault.

Major fault

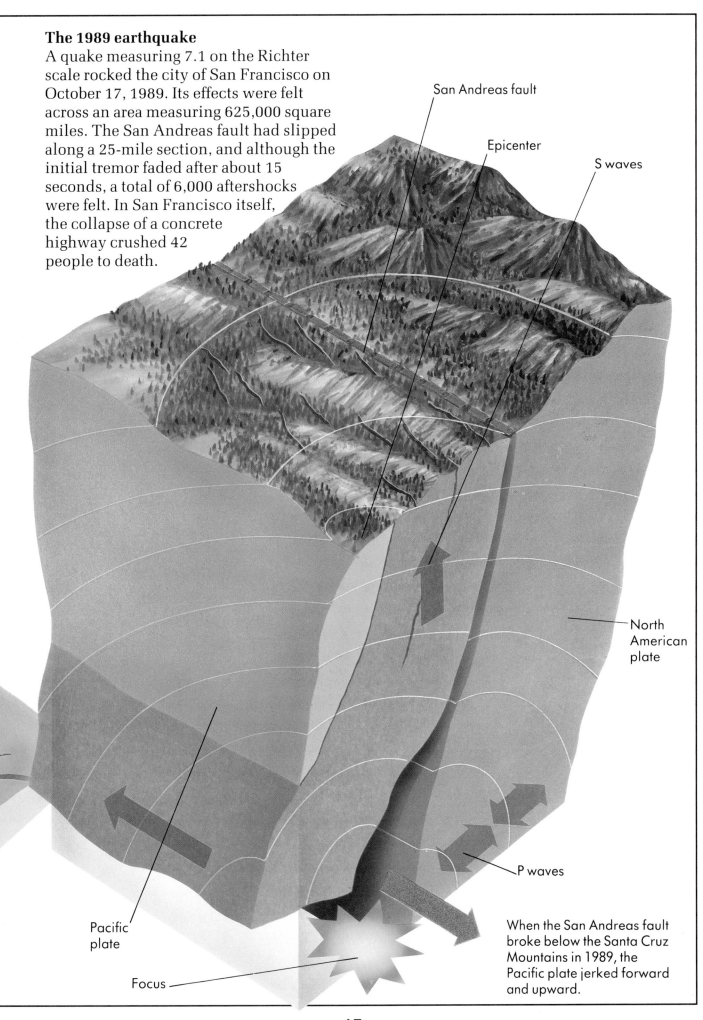

The 1989 earthquake

A quake measuring 7.1 on the Richter scale rocked the city of San Francisco on October 17, 1989. Its effects were felt across an area measuring 625,000 square miles. The San Andreas fault had slipped along a 25-mile section, and although the initial tremor faded after about 15 seconds, a total of 6,000 aftershocks were felt. In San Francisco itself, the collapse of a concrete highway crushed 42 people to death.

San Andreas fault

Epicenter

S waves

North American plate

P waves

Pacific plate

Focus

When the San Andreas fault broke below the Santa Cruz Mountains in 1989, the Pacific plate jerked forward and upward.

EARTHQUAKES TODAY

Each year, an estimated 500,000 disturbances occur within the earth's crust. Most pass unnoticed, but about 1,000 earthquakes a year cause some damage, and occasionally a major earthquake brings disaster. At 11:41 a.m. on December 7, 1988, an earthquake (Richter scale 7.0) struck the Republic of Armenia in the Soviet Union. The small town of Spitak lay in ruins, while in nearby Leninakan and Kirovakan, up to three-quarters of all buildings were destroyed. After an initial estimate of 55,000, the death toll was revised down to 25,000.

Deep below the surface of the Caspian Sea, on June 21, 1990, shock waves were released from the focus of an earthquake measuring between 7.3 and 7.7 on the Richter scale. The first tremor was felt in the Iranian capital of Tehran. A second one followed 12 hours later.

In October 1991, a series of four earthquakes in northern India left more than 500 people dead and thousands injured. The most powerful quake measured 7.1 on the Richter scale. Its epicenter was around the town of Uttarkarshi, but tremors were felt in the Indian capital of Delhi 150 miles away. Rescue operations were hampered by the mountainous landscape, and by landslides which blocked a tributary of the River Ganges.

▼ A tangled heap of twisted metal and broken concrete marks the site of a 16-story building that collapsed after the 1989 earthquake in Armenia.

Relief efforts

After the recent earthquakes in the Soviet Union and Iran, huge international relief operations were mounted to help these countries handle such disasters. In Armenia, freezing winter conditions, uncoordinated relief efforts, and damage to the area's road and rail networks hampered the rescue operation. In Iran, the mountainous terrain proved to be an obstacle in reaching people in stricken villages.

◀ After the 1985 earthquake in Mexico City (Richter scale 8.1), a lack of basic equipment, such as cranes and saws to cut through concrete, prevented volunteers from freeing people trapped under the rubble of collapsed buildings.

◀◀ The worst effects of the 1990 Iranian earthquake centered on the towns of Binab and Abhor, both of which were destroyed. About 35,000 people were killed, and thousands more were injured.

EARTHQUAKE PREDICTION

On the afternoon of February 4, 1974, a radio broadcast to the three million inhabitants of Liaoning Province in China warned them to leave their homes immediately because of an impending earthquake. Just after 7:30 that evening, an earthquake destroyed or damaged almost all the buildings in the city of Haicheng (pop. 90,000). Miraculously, the death toll was only about 300 people. For the first time anywhere in the world an earthquake of this strength had been predicted correctly.

Seismologists have identified several warning signs in the buildup to an earthquake: alterations in the speed of seismic waves, swellings in the ground and a large number of minor tremors along the plate boundaries. With the help of modern technology, scientists can monitor even the tiniest movement in the earth's plates. Scientists in China have relied on a number of less scientific warning signs to predict earthquakes. They claim that, before an earthquake, fish become very agitated and small animals like mice and rabbits run around in panic.

The picture on the right shows a scientist checking the equipment installed in one of 18 water wells around the town of Parkfield in California. Situated along the San Andreas fault, scientists predicted that an earthquake would occur there, as it did early in 1994. Dozens of researchers made the town of Parkfield their most closely-monitored earth-quake region in the world. Instruments in the wells record the level of groundwater as the rock beneath is affected by the buildup of pressure caused by seismic activity. The antenna situated on top of the equipment transmits data to a satellite which then relays the information to Parkfield Experiment Headquaters for analysis.

▶ A creepmeter measures the continuous horizontal movement along a fault line. A weight on the end of a piece of wire rises or falls as the fault moves.

▼ The black "trash can" shown below is the covering of a well containing a strain meter. Strain meters can detect even tiny rock movements. The solar panels provide energy to operate the equipment.

Laser light

The United States and Japan have been world leaders in developing new technology to help predict earthquakes. Some American monitoring stations use laser beams to detect any movement in the rocks beneath the ground. A beam of laser light is sent from one side of a fault line to a reflector positioned on the opposite side. By calculating the amount of time it takes the laser beam to bounce off the reflector, scientists can measure any movement of the ground that occurs along the fault.

51

WHAT CAN WE DO?

We do not yet know how to prevent earthquakes, so how can we make sure that they cause as little damage and as few deaths as possible?

Cities and towns in earthquake zones should be carefully planned and designed. Gas and water pipes and electricity cables should be well protected. In some earthquake-prone areas in the United States, electricity generators automatically shut down in the event of an earthquake, and gas pipes are closed by automatic valves. Other countries are also taking protective measures. In Iran, reinforced brick structures are replacing flat-roofed mud homes, and in Tashkent in the Soviet Union concrete buildings have replaced the brick and mud structures.

The 837 ft-high Transamerica Building in San Francisco (pictured below) is a monument to the success of earthquake architecture. Its triangular framework is supported by concrete-clad steel columns which should withstand even the most severe earthquake.

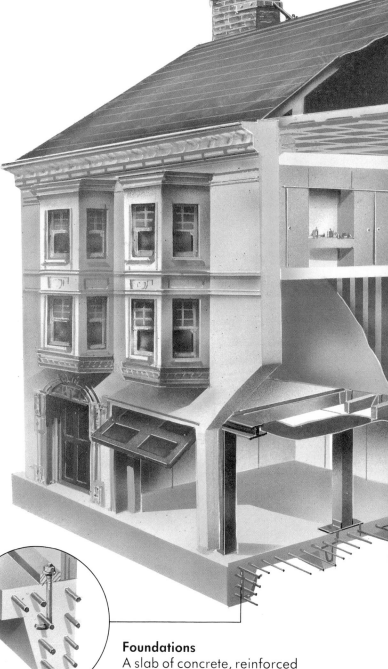

Foundations
A slab of concrete, reinforced with steel rods, will support the building. The walls are reinforced by securing them to the foundations with anchor bolts.

Chimneys
Brick chimneys must be secured with special brackets. Metal ones are lighter and cause less damage.

An earthquake-resistant house should be a low structure made of reinforced concrete. There should be strong walls on the first storey, where the effects of the quake are greatest. Foundations should be deep or flexible so that the building can sway as the ground beneath it shakes during a tremor. It is better to build on solid rock such as granite. Clay, sand and other soft surfaces increase the effects of the seismic waves.

Beams and joists
Extra reinforcement is essential where wall beams and floor joists join up. The house must be able to withstand both the vertical and the horizontal shaking movements experienced during an earthquake.

▼ The wide streets of San Francisco help to prevent the spread of fire during an earthquake, and also allow buildings to sway, without crashing into each other.

Water heater
Boilers, generators, and water heaters are firmly secured to prevent them breaking loose and fracturing gas pipes.

FACTFILE: *Earthquakes*

The worst death toll

The largest number of deaths from an earthquake was believed to have occurred around July 1201. The earthquake affected the Near East and eastern Mediterranean regions, leaving an estimated 1.1 million dead.

An earthquake in the Chinese city of Tangshan in 1976 measured 7.9 on the Richter scale. The death toll was originally believed to be about 650,000, but was later reduced to 242,000 by the Chinese Government.

Largest earthquake

An earthquake measuring 8.9 on the Richter scale struck Alaska on Good Friday, March 27, 1964. The damage caused by the quake was estimated at $750 million. Five hours after the first tremor, a giant *tsunami* demolished the Alaskan port of Valdez, while at the oil port of Seward, a 33 ft wave topped with burning oil surged across the dockside, sweeping away all the port's facilities.

Historical patterns

Scientists cannot ignore historical patterns when predicting earthquakes in some quake-prone areas. In Mexico, where five times as many earthquakes occur each year as in California, a major earthquake occurs every 35 years. The strength of the shock waves unleashed by the 1985 quake there was 1,000 times more powerful than the atomic bomb that destroyed Hiroshima in Japan at the end of World War II.

In the small town of Parkfield, midway between Los Angeles and San Francisco, an earthquake occurs every 20 years. Cameras have been installed in a local bar in the town to record the event of the next earthquake. In San Francisco, scientists predict a strong possibility of a major earthquake occurring before the year 2020.

San Francisco, 1989

The focus of the 1989 earthquake was 11 miles below the peak of Loma Prieta in the Santa Cruz Mountains. This was the 11th earthquake measuring 5.3 or more on the Richter scale to strike the area of San Francisco Bay since 1865.

Recent earthquakes 1990

Peru (Richter scale 5.8) 100 people killed and hundreds missing. Villages in the forest region of San Martín were flattened or swallowed up by landslides. Romania (Richter scale 6.5-7.0) earthquake centered around town of Focsani, north-east of the capital Bucharest. About 70 people were killed, but the damage was limited as it was an intermediate-focus quake, occurring 60-90 miles below the surface.

Philippines (Richter scale 7.7) over 1,500 dead, 3,000 seriously injured and 110,000 homeless after an earthquake in northern Philippines. In the tourist resort of Baguio, hundreds of people were trapped under the rubble of collapsed buildings. 14 days after the first tremor, a man was rescued from beneath the rubble of a hotel.

1991

Pakistan (Richter scale 6.8) 300 dead and 500 injured in North West Frontier Province. Severe damage to homes, roads, and power and telephone lines. Afghanistan (Richter scale 6.5-6.8) epicenter in Hindu Kush Mountains, affecting remote villages of northern and eastern Afghanistan and killing 1,000 people. Central America (Richter scale 7.5) earthquake in border area between Costa Rica and Panama destroyed thousands of homes, leaving 80 dead and 800 injured. Soviet Union (Richter scale 7.2) in northern Georgia, this earthquake caused damage in the Republic's second largest city, Kutaisi, and in remote villages, leaving 100 dead.

First Australian quake

The first fatal earthquake (Richter scale 5.5) ever recorded in Australia hit the town of Newcastle in New South Wales on December 28, 1989, killing 12 people and injuring 120.

Chapter Three

AVALANCHES
AND LANDSLIDES

CONTENTS

INTRODUCTION

A huge mass of snow, rock, or mud crashes down from a mountain or hillside at high speed. It can engulf and destroy entire towns and villages in minutes. With a thunderous roar, avalanches and landslides strike quickly and often without warning, and their impact can be catastrophic.

Hundreds of avalanches occur each day on remote snowy mountaintops throughout the world. However, their effect is only really felt in the populated mountain regions. Here, the whirling mass of ice and snow will crush to death or bury alive any person or animal unlucky enough to be caught in its path.

The introduction of improved warning systems can reduce the effects of avalanches and landslides. But we must also try to control the human activities that can trigger these natural disasters.

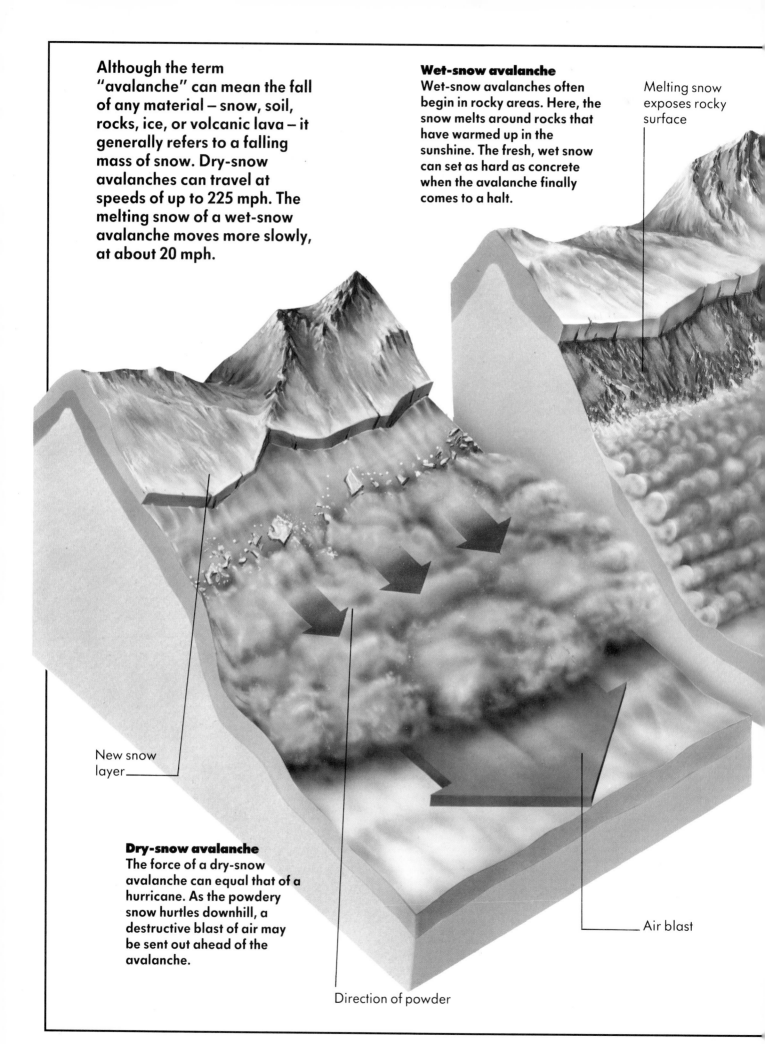

Although the term "avalanche" can mean the fall of any material – snow, soil, rocks, ice, or volcanic lava – it generally refers to a falling mass of snow. Dry-snow avalanches can travel at speeds of up to 225 mph. The melting snow of a wet-snow avalanche moves more slowly, at about 20 mph.

Wet-snow avalanche

Wet-snow avalanches often begin in rocky areas. Here, the snow melts around rocks that have warmed up in the sunshine. The fresh, wet snow can set as hard as concrete when the avalanche finally comes to a halt.

Melting snow exposes rocky surface

New snow layer

Dry-snow avalanche

The force of a dry-snow avalanche can equal that of a hurricane. As the powdery snow hurtles downhill, a destructive blast of air may be sent out ahead of the avalanche.

Air blast

Direction of powder

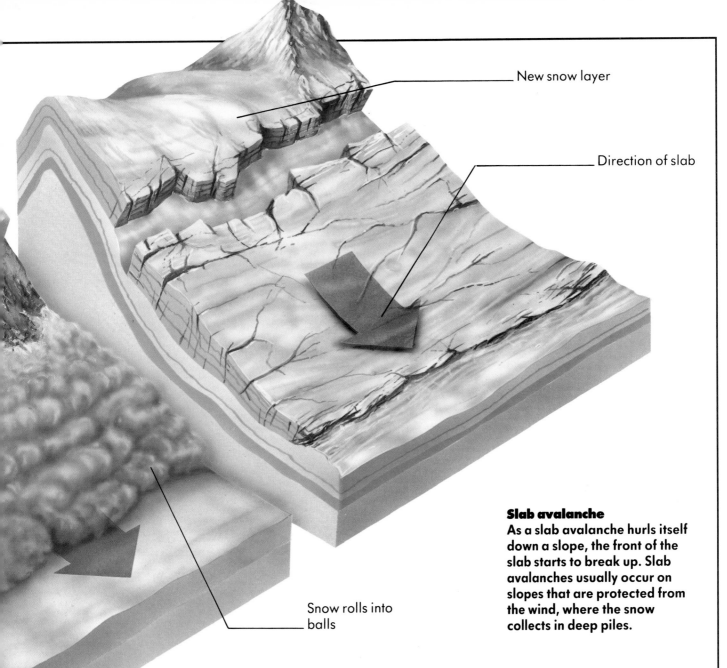

New snow layer

Direction of slab

Slab avalanche
As a slab avalanche hurls itself down a slope, the front of the slab starts to break up. Slab avalanches usually occur on slopes that are protected from the wind, where the snow collects in deep piles.

Snow rolls into balls

WHAT IS AN AVALANCHE?

An avalanche is a huge mass of ice and snow which breaks away from the side of a mountain and surges downward at great speed. The greatest avalanches probably occur on the high peaks of the Himalayas. However, those which cause the highest death toll fall in the populated valleys of the Alps.

Scientists have grouped avalanches into three main kinds: wet-snow avalanche, dry-snow avalanche, and slab avalanche. Wet-snow avalanches usually occur in the spring, when the loose, melting snow forms into large boulders of snow as it rolls downhill. More deadly are the dry-snow avalanches, which either slide along close to the ground, or lift off the ground completely and swirl through the air, often hundreds of feet high. In a slab avalanche, a huge chunk of solid, sticky snow breaks away from a slope. It slides across a layer of loose snow crystals lying beneath the surface.

AN AVALANCHE BEGINS

Most avalanches begin either during or soon after a snowstorm. As each new layer of snow settles on the ground, it binds itself to the existing layers that are anchored to the mountainside. The additional weight of a heavy snowfall can prevent the snow from gripping onto the layers of snow underneath, and trigger an avalanche. Avalanches also occur during the spring, when melting snow seeps down through the surface. This creates a slippery layer on which the snow can slide.

The steepness of the slope can also affect the speed of the avalanche. Steep, rocky slopes help to anchor the snow. The smooth surface of gentler grass-covered slopes allows the avalanche to reach great speeds.

Heavy snowfalls
The weight from deep piles of falling or drifting snow can produce an avalanche.

Explosions
An avalanche can be set in motion by an explosion at a mine or quarry, by the noise of a low-flying plane, or even by a clap of thunder.

Avalanches are not only caused by natural factors, such as the amount and quality of the snow, or the sudden arrival of strong winds. Once conditions are suitable, an avalanche can be started by the slightest movement, such as a falling icicle or twig, or by a small animal crossing a slope.

Cornices
Hard winds drive the snow and pack it together to form a cornice, which hangs over the very top of the slope. When a cornice falls, it can trigger an avalanche.

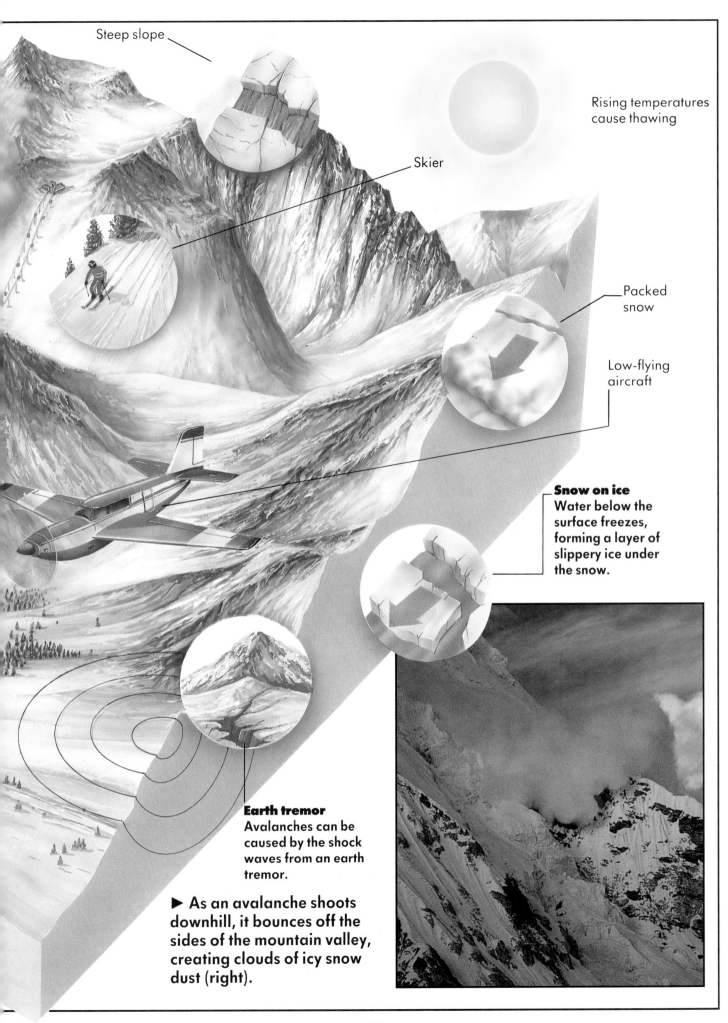

Steep slope

Rising temperatures
cause thawing

Skier

Packed
snow

Low-flying
aircraft

Snow on ice
Water below the
surface freezes,
forming a layer of
slippery ice under
the snow.

Earth tremor
Avalanches can be
caused by the shock
waves from an earth
tremor.

▶ As an avalanche shoots
downhill, it bounces off the
sides of the mountain valley,
creating clouds of icy snow
dust (right).

THE WHITE DEATH

When an avalanche strikes, more than 130 million cubic yards of snow and ice blast down a mountainside. As the ice mass falls, it collects large amounts of debris such as rocks and tree stumps on its way. In a populated mountain area, whole villages are crushed, hundreds of people and animals are buried alive, power and water supplies are cut off, and roads and railroad lines disappear – all in a matter of minutes.

The world's greatest single avalanche disaster occurred in 1962 in Peru. More than 3,500 people died and eight villages and towns were destroyed in just 7 minutes. When the avalanche finally came to rest, after a journey of almost 10 miles, the pile of snow and ice was over 60 feet deep.

Trapped under the hard, packed snow, an avalanche victim can barely move and is unlikely to survive for more than a couple of hours. Victims die from the cold, from a lack of oxygen, or from the injuries that occurred when they were first struck. Only about 5 percent of all avalanche victims are rescued alive.

6:18 p.m.
The deadly torrent of ice and rocks misses Yungay, but crushes the village of Ranrahirca, killing 2,700 people.

◄ In the mountain village shown left, a path has been cut through the wall of snow and debris caused by a recent avalanche.

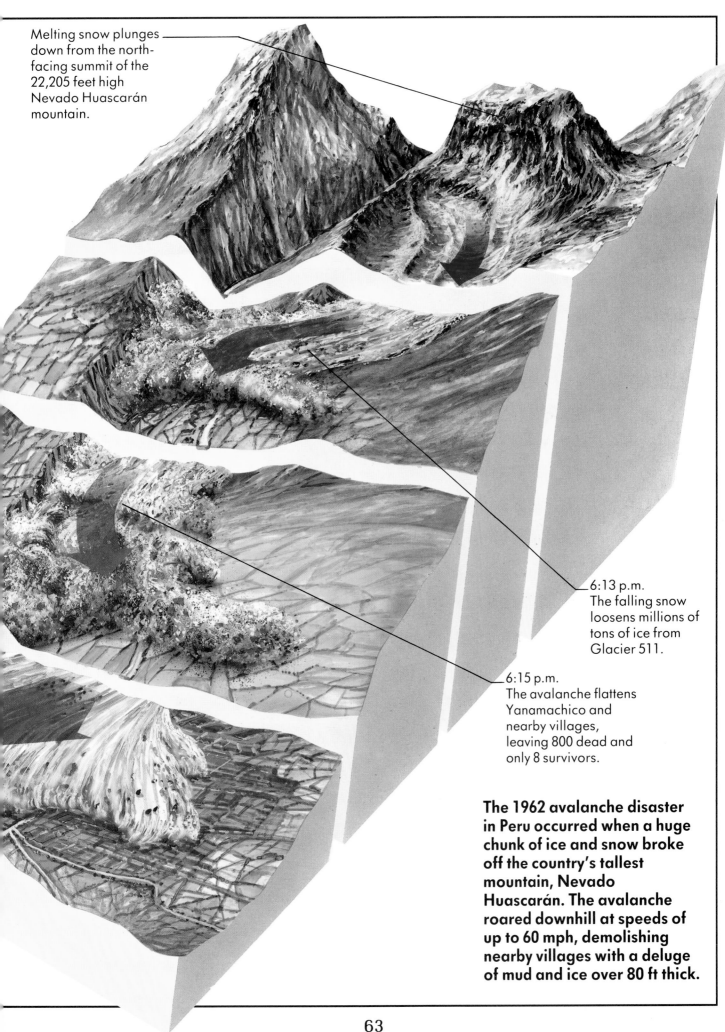

Melting snow plunges down from the north-facing summit of the 22,205 feet high Nevado Huascarán mountain.

6:13 p.m.
The falling snow loosens millions of tons of ice from Glacier 511.

6:15 p.m.
The avalanche flattens Yanamachico and nearby villages, leaving 800 dead and only 8 survivors.

The 1962 avalanche disaster in Peru occurred when a huge chunk of ice and snow broke off the country's tallest mountain, Nevado Huascarán. The avalanche roared downhill at speeds of up to 60 mph, demolishing nearby villages with a deluge of mud and ice over 80 ft thick.

THE ALPS

Each year, tens of thousands of avalanches occur in the European Alps, the world's most densely populated mountain region. The inhabitants of the numerous Alpine towns and villages live under the constant threat of avalanches, which is made worse by certain natural conditions that prevail there.

The warm dry Föhn wind which blows through the deep Alpine valleys raises temperatures suddenly, causing the snows to melt rapidly. The smooth surface of the Alpine meadows lubricates the path of the avalanches, which travel at terrifying speeds. In 1898, an avalanche at Glärnisch in Switzerland raced downhill at around 250 mph.

During the 1950-51 "Winter of Terror" in Switzerland, over 1,100 avalanches killed a total of 98 people.

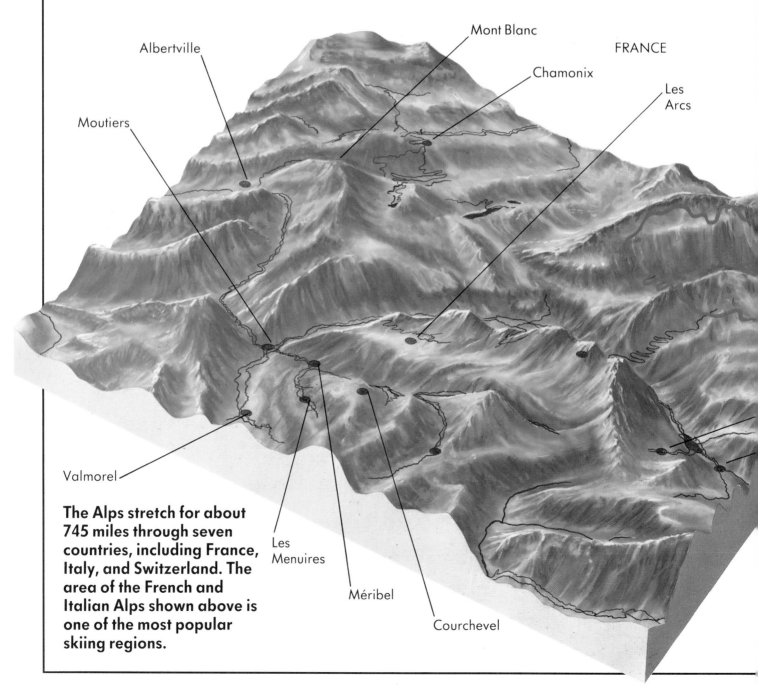

The Alps stretch for about 745 miles through seven countries, including France, Italy, and Switzerland. The area of the French and Italian Alps shown above is one of the most popular skiing regions.

64

◄ Avalanche warning signs, such as the one shown left, inform skiers if there is a danger of avalanches. The ski trails, called pistes, that are at risk are then closed.

Experienced skiers who choose to ski "off piste" on unmarked trails run the risk of setting off an avalanche. The weight of a single skier on a slope can open up a crack in the hard crust on the snow's surface. This releases a huge slab which breaks away, often at a point above the skier, offering little chance of escape.

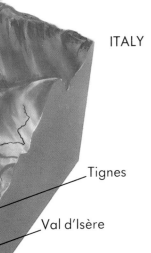

ITALY

Tignes

Val d'Isère

► More and more people visit the Alps each year. New hotels, ski lifts, electricity lines, and roads are being built to meet the increased demand for facilities. Avalanches in these developed areas are now more likely to cause widespread damage and many deaths.

WHAT ARE LANDSLIDES?

A landslide is the name given to the downhill movement of large amounts of soil, mud, rocks, and other debris. There are three different kinds of landslide: falls, slides, and flows.

In a rockfall, huge boulders crash down a steep slope, often breaking up into smaller pieces on reaching the ground. When rockslides occur, the chunks of rocky material slide over the ground as quickly as flowing water. Debris slides, which consist of thin layers of loose soil and smaller rocks, travel in the same way.

Mudflows and earthflows are wet landslides. A mass of mud and water flows down from the upper slopes, picking up debris lying in its path.

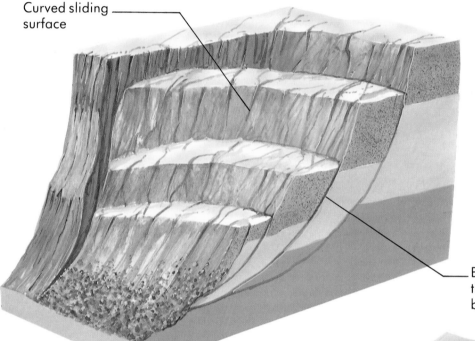

Curved sliding surface

Slump
A slump occurs when heavy rock and soil on a steep slope or cliff collapse in a series of curving movements. The blocks of slumped material tilt back toward the slope.

Blocks tilt backward

Rockslide
Rockslides involve the downward movement of rock debris or large blocks of rock. They often occur after heavy rains and in areas where large numbers of trees have been removed from the slopes.

Large blocks become detached from slope.

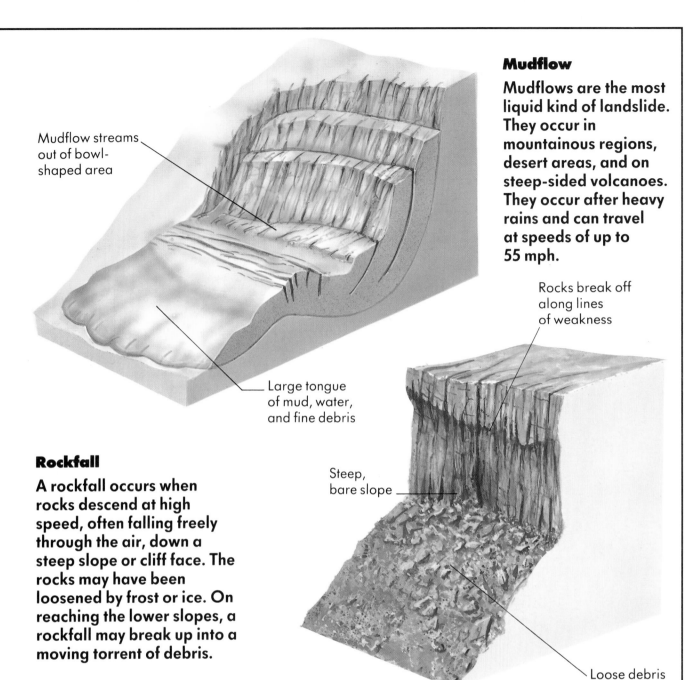

Mudflow streams out of bowl-shaped area

Mudflow

Mudflows are the most liquid kind of landslide. They occur in mountainous regions, desert areas, and on steep-sided volcanoes. They occur after heavy rains and can travel at speeds of up to 55 mph.

Large tongue of mud, water, and fine debris

Rocks break off along lines of weakness

Rockfall

A rockfall occurs when rocks descend at high speed, often falling freely through the air, down a steep slope or cliff face. The rocks may have been loosened by frost or ice. On reaching the lower slopes, a rockfall may break up into a moving torrent of debris.

Steep, bare slope

Loose debris on slope

Flooding

Flooding is a common aftereffect of landslides. The debris from a landslide can fill a riverbed. The river may then burst its banks, causing flooding (right).

In Utah, in 1982-83 heavy rains caused a huge mudslide that damned Spanish Folk Canyon. A lake of water was created, which drowned the nearby town of Thistle.

LANDSLIDE CAUSES

A landslide begins when the loose material on the surface of a slope becomes unstable. Water is one of the key factors in triggering landslides. After heavy rainfall or melting snow, the surface soil becomes saturated. Water seeps through the top layer, making the layers underneath very slippery. The water increases the weight of the surface material – soil, small rocks, and sediment – and weakens the forces that bind it.

As the soil loses its grip on the slope, it can no longer resist the downward pull of gravity. On steep slopes, the water-filled mass forms into a slide. On gentler slopes, it becomes a flow of earth and debris.

Erosion, where the lower layers of a slope are cut or worn away, is another major cause of landslides. Erosion can result from natural factors, such as the action of the sea or rivers, or from artificial ones, such as mining and excavating. A landslide itself can be a major force of erosion, especially on steep slopes where the tree cover has been removed.

Landslides are also associated with earthquakes and volcanic activity. After the devastating earthquake in 1964 in the state of Alaska much of the destruction resulted from landslides.

The upper slopes of this valley have slipped downward in a landslide. The river that flowed through the valley wore away the lower slopes, leaving the upper ones without support.

▼ **In the Trisuli Valley in Nepal (below), the soil has been eroded from the steep mountainsides. This erosion is partly due to tree-felling operations in the area.**

Water-soaked layers of shale help to lubricate the landslide.

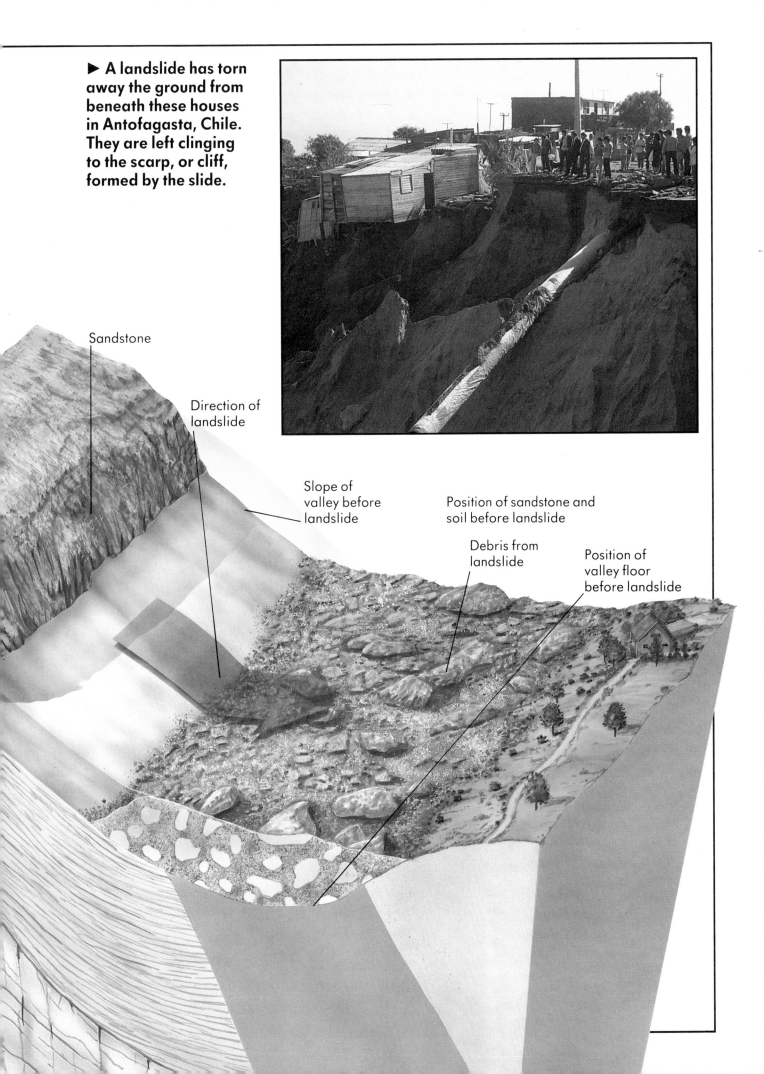

► A landslide has torn away the ground from beneath these houses in Antofagasta, Chile. They are left clinging to the scarp, or cliff, formed by the slide.

Sandstone

Direction of landslide

Slope of valley before landslide

Position of sandstone and soil before landslide

Debris from landslide

Position of valley floor before landslide

DISASTER STRIKES

When a landslide begins its descent, huge quantities of soil, mud, rocks, and smaller debris hurtle down a hillside. Whole villages are buried alive, and their inhabitants and livestock are swept along on a tide of mud and debris. Trees are uprooted, houses are flattened or swamped, and communications are cut off.

The mountainous regions of Nepal in Asia are prone to torrential rains. Here, the water-saturated soil has been eroded, exposing the layers of rock beneath. This erosion is worse in areas where large numbers of trees have been cut down. The hillsides are stripped of protection against the falling rain, and of tree roots to anchor the soil in place. Landslides glide over the smooth rock at speeds of up to 60 feet per second.

Following an earthquake in the Andes Mountains in Peru in 1970, a devastating mudflow swept through the Peruvian town of Yungay. Almost 18,000 people were buried alive as a giant wave of mud and debris about 263 feet high swamped the town.

▶▲▲ Shockwaves from the 1964 Alaska earthquake caused a mudflow of clay to engulf the town.
▶▲ Mud and floodwaters wreaked havoc in the streets of Armero, Colombia, after the 1985 volcanic eruption there.
▶ The 1970 mudflow in Yungay, Peru, caused severe damage to railroad lines and roads (right).

Torrential rains

San Gabriel Mountains

Direction of mudflow

Glendora

◄ In 1969, in the area around Los Angeles, about 44 inches of rain fell in just 42 days. These rains, some of the heaviest ever recorded in the area, washed down mud and gravel from the San Gabriel Mountains. As a torrent of mud, debris, and water swept over the suburb of Glendora, over 100 people were drowned and 15,000 people had to evacuate their homes. The landslide also blocked the main highway into Los Angeles.

LOOKING BACK

Evidence of avalanches and landslides dating back to prehistoric times can still be seen today. On the floor of the Saidmarreh Valley, in western Iran, lie the remains of a landslide that scientists believe occurred over 2,000 years ago. Limestone debris covers an area of around 77 square miles, and is 985 feet deep in places.

In 218 B.C., Hannibal and his army suffered huge losses from avalanches as they crossed the Alps on their way from Carthage to attack Rome. It was October, and fresh snow had fallen on a crust of old snow. Thousands of troops and animals were carried away by the avalanches triggered off as they crossed the unstable crust.

In the Middle Ages, pilgrims from northern Europe regularly crossed the Alps on their way to worship in Rome. Many believed that avalanches were acts of God, while others thought they showed the destructive power of the devil.

Landslide!
On the morning of Christmas Day, 1839, a gaping hole opened up in the top of the cliffs at Bindon in Devon, England (left). A vast chunk of rock sank down, leaving an enormous gap about 4,000 feet long and 300 feet wide. The steep slope, or scarp, down which the landslide moved, is still visible today, as are the huge lumps of displaced rock.

▶ During the winters of World War I (1914-18), an estimated 60,000 soldiers fighting in the Alps were killed by avalanches. Some of these avalanches were not entirely due to natural causes. After a heavy snowfall, Austrian and Italian troops often fired into the slopes on top of the enemy below. This action released huge dry-snow avalanches. It was the first time in military history that avalanches had been used as a weapon.

◀ Hannibal's treacherous journey across the Alps involved about 38,000 foot soldiers, 8,000 horses, and over 30 elephants. According to the Roman historian Livius, more than 18,000 men and 2,000 horses were lost during the crossing, mainly because of avalanches. The reduced numbers of Hannibal's troops contributed to their eventual defeat by the Roman army.

ARE WE CAUSING MORE?

We cannot prevent natural disasters such as avalanches and landslides. Yet we can stop or reduce the human activities that make it more likely that one of these powerful forces will strike. When large numbers of trees are cut down, to provide fuel and lumber, as well as land for farming, nothing remains to trap the rainwater and hold the surface of the slopes in place. This deforestation also removes the natural barrier to avalanches and landslides that trees and other vegetation provide.

Mountainous areas in other parts of the world are also being cleared and developed as tourist resorts. Millions of people then visit the mountains to sightsee and explore. These activities can wear away the soil and vegetation, making the area more prone to avalanches and landslides.

Road construction
Excavation work for new road building steepens slopes and removes support for the upper layers.

Quarrying and mining
As large amounts of natural resources, such as stone and coal, are removed from the ground, the surrounding land becomes unstable and may collapse.

Deforestation
The roots of trees and ground foliage hold water like a sponge, releasing it slowly into the surrounding soil in a controlled flow. When a hillside is stripped of its cover, the exposed soil erodes very quickly.

The threat of landslides and avalanches is increased by excavation and construction work, and by the removal of natural resources from the ground. The shape of a slope may be steepened or altered to such an extent that it becomes unstable. Heavy rains and snow add further weight to the slope, weakening the surface soil's grip on the hillside.

Reservoirs
The construction of reservoirs in narrow mountain valleys that are prone to landslides increases the risk of a flood disaster.

▲ Trees help to prevent the erosion of soil by heavy rains. Deforestation has caused this landslide in Malaysia (above). The slide has completely destroyed a main road.

Forest fires
A lack of hillside vegetation is blamed for the mudflows that are common in parts of southern California. Forest fires destroy the trees and shrubs on the steep slopes around many residential areas. After heavy rains, the topsoil on the slopes becomes saturated with water and starts to slip downhill.

Global warming
As the atmosphere traps increasing amounts of the greenhouse gases that warm the earth, changes in weather patterns may occur. Very heavy rains could increase the number of mudflows and landslides.

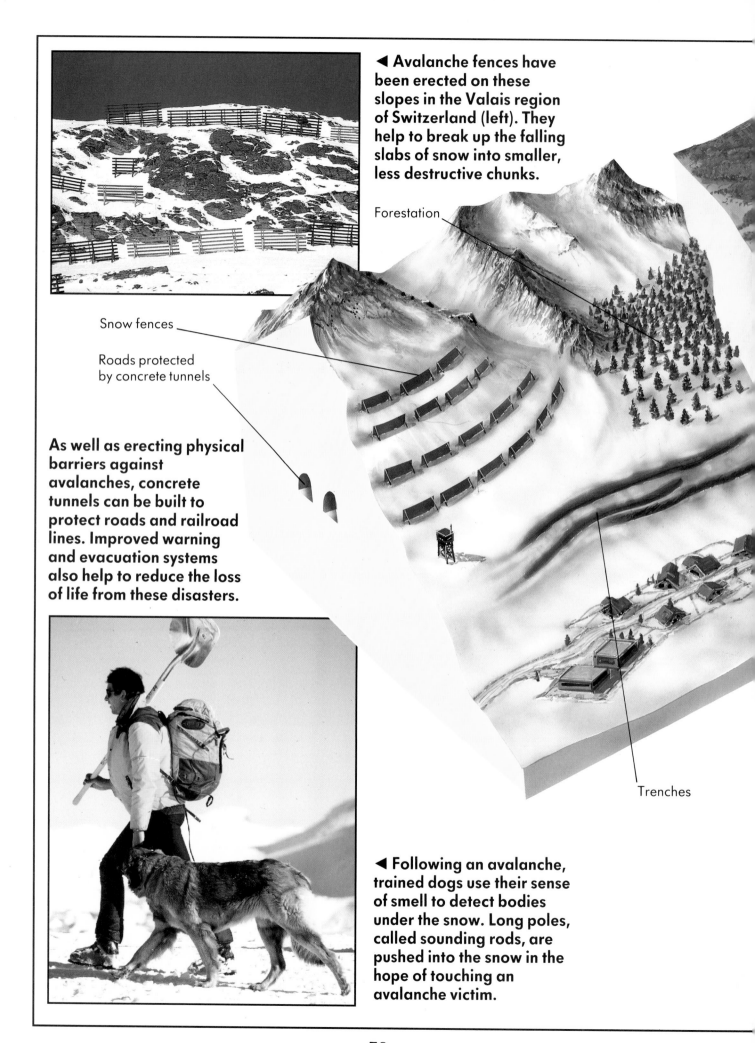

◄ Avalanche fences have been erected on these slopes in the Valais region of Switzerland (left). They help to break up the falling slabs of snow into smaller, less destructive chunks.

Forestation

Snow fences

Roads protected by concrete tunnels

As well as erecting physical barriers against avalanches, concrete tunnels can be built to protect roads and railroad lines. Improved warning and evacuation systems also help to reduce the loss of life from these disasters.

Trenches

◄ Following an avalanche, trained dogs use their sense of smell to detect bodies under the snow. Long poles, called sounding rods, are pushed into the snow in the hope of touching an avalanche victim.

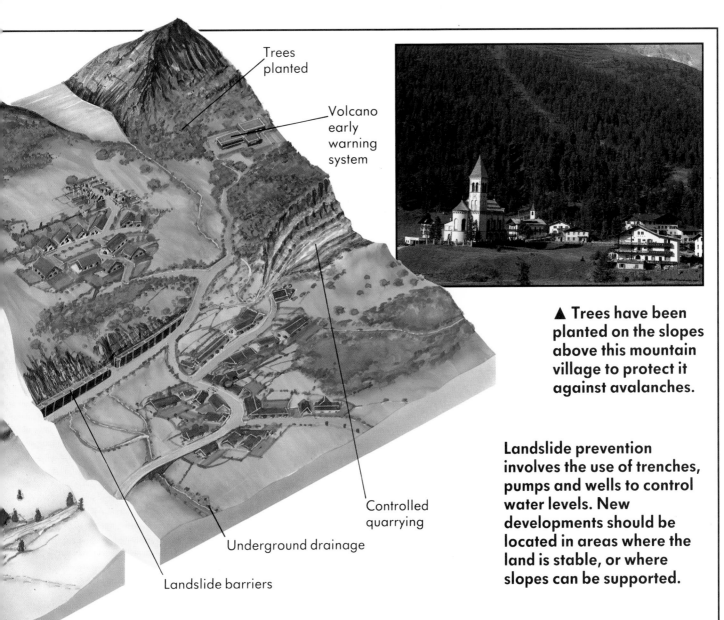

Trees planted

Volcano early warning system

Controlled quarrying

Underground drainage

Landslide barriers

▲ Trees have been planted on the slopes above this mountain village to protect it against avalanches.

Landslide prevention involves the use of trenches, pumps and wells to control water levels. New developments should be located in areas where the land is stable, or where slopes can be supported.

WHAT CAN WE DO?

Many different measures can be taken to reduce the devastating impact of an avalanche or landslide. In Switzerland, controls include setting off explosives to release avalanches artificially, and planting triangular patches of trees above mountain villages. Antiavalanche constructions, such as trees, fences, or barriers, are used to slow down, deflect, or break up the falling snow.

Water is one of the prime causes of landslides. Measures can be taken to control and monitor the amount and pressure of the water in unstable slopes. Underground drainage is also installed in some places to reduce the water content of landslide-prone hillsides. The lower end, or toe, of a slide can be shored up with concrete, rock or soil.

In the United States, scientists are using computers to try and forecast avalanches. The study of volcanoes can also help to predict volcanic eruptions more accurately, thus reducing the death toll from volcanic mudflows.

FACTFILE: *Avalanches & Landslides*

The world's largest landslide

The largest landslide in the world in the past 2 million years is believed to have occurred in the United States. At the foot of Mount Shasta, an active volcano in the state of California, lies an area of debris covering some 175 square miles. The debris is believed to date from a rockfall that happened between 300,000 and 360,000 years ago.

Recent avalanches and landslides
1990
Peru – following heavy rains, a mudslide buried the village of San Miguel de Río Mayo in the jungle region 500 mi north of the capital, Lima. A total of 200 people were reported missing.

1991
Malawi, Southeast Africa – after flooding and a series of mudslides in the southeast of the country in March, 516 were reported dead or missing, and over 40,000 people were left homeless.

New Zealand – a huge avalanche on December 14 almost destroyed the eastern face of Mount Cook, the highest mountain in New Zealand. Thousands of tons of ice, snow, and rock hurtled down from the summit of the 12,350-foot high mountain, and smashed into the Tasman Glacier, a popular tourist spot, over 4 miles below.

1992
Argentina – torrential rain in January caused a debris avalanche of rocks, mud, and trees to destroy the town of San Carlos Minas. Sixty people were believed to have been killed.

Turkey – avalanches in February in the remote Kurdish Mountains of southeastern Turkey left more than 150 people dead. In the village of Gormec, 71 soldiers died under a single avalanche. Rescue workers were delayed by blocked roads and strong blizzards.

Israel – tons of rocks and soil fell on a cafe in East Jerusalem on February 29, leaving 23 people dead and a further 20 injured. After heavy snow and rain, part of the hillside above the café collapsed and burst through a wall onto the café below.

Avalanche control in Canada

In Canada's Selkirk Mountains, one of the world's largest anti-avalanche programs is operated along Rogers Pass, with the help of the Royal Canadian Horse Artillery. In a densely populated mountain area, the soldiers use gunfire to release avalanches and protect a 25-mile stretch of major road from 160 separate avalanche paths.

Mudflow technology

Japan has become a world leader in the study and prevention of mudflows. Since 10 percent of the world's active volcanoes are found in Japan, many of the country's population centers are threatened by mudflows. On the side of Mount Usu on the island of Hokkaido, steel and concrete structures have been erected to trap falling rocks and slow down the flow of mud and other debris. Elsewhere, television monitors and measuring equipment help to detect volcanic activity and the onset of a mudflow or other landslide.

Volcanic mudflows

On the slopes of Mount Rainier, a volcano in Washington state, more than 55 mudflows have been recorded in the past 10,000 years.

Landslide deaths

Between 25 and 50 people die in the United States each year from landslides.

Mining waste disaster

The waste material from mining and excavating can be a serious landslide hazard. For many years, the waste from the coal mines around Aberfan in South Wales was piled dangerously high. When it became saturated with water following heavy rains in October 1966, part of the trash heap collapsed. The waste material slid downhill, killing over 144 people including 116 children in the local school.

Chapter Four

HURRICANES
AND TYPHOONS

CONTENTS

INTRODUCTION

Hurricanes, typhoons, and cyclones are the names given to massive tropical storms in different parts of the world. Tropical storms differ from ordinary storms in several important respects. For example, the winds in a tropical storm are always rotational. They whirl around in a circular motion at speeds far greater than those in any ordinary storm. In addition, while the energy unleashed by an ordinary storm is sufficient to provide the whole of the United States with power for 20 minutes, the energy unleashed by a tropical storm is 12,000 times as powerful. Such terrible power has brought death and destruction to many areas of the world, as was shown by the cyclone that battered Bangladesh in April 1991, killing over 250,000 people.

THE WORLD'S WINDS

Winds are caused by movements of warm and cold air. Warm air is lighter than cold air, so it rises, creating an area of low pressure at the earth's surface. In other places cold air sinks down toward the earth's surface, and spreads out to create an area of high pressure. Winds are therefore movements of air over the earth's surface from areas of high pressure to areas of low pressure.

At the equator, where the sun's rays are strongest, warm air is constantly rising, which leads to areas of low pressure. At the poles, the sun's rays are weaker. Air is cooled over the icy polar caps, and sinks to create areas of high pressure. Around the earth, movements of air between areas of high and low pressure result in the convection cells (right).

The winds are complicated by the spinning of the earth, which bends the flows of air clockwise in the northern hemisphere and counterclockwise in the southern hemisphere. This is known as the Coriolis effect.

▼ **This map shows the prevailing global winds and the breeding grounds in which tropical storms can develop (shaded areas).**

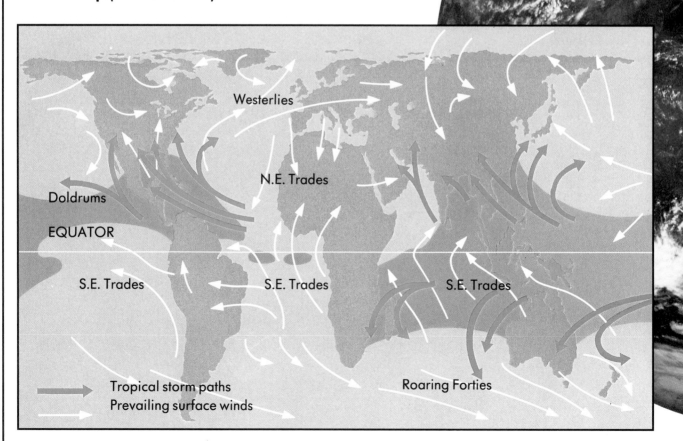

Westerlies

N.E. Trades

Doldrums

EQUATOR

S.E. Trades

S.E. Trades

S.E. Trades

Roaring Forties

→ Tropical storm paths
→ Prevailing surface winds

82

Wind cells

The heating effect of the sun on the earth's surface results in three massive "cells" of rising and falling air. At the earth's surface, winds blowing from high pressure to low pressure areas are bent by the Coriolis effect.

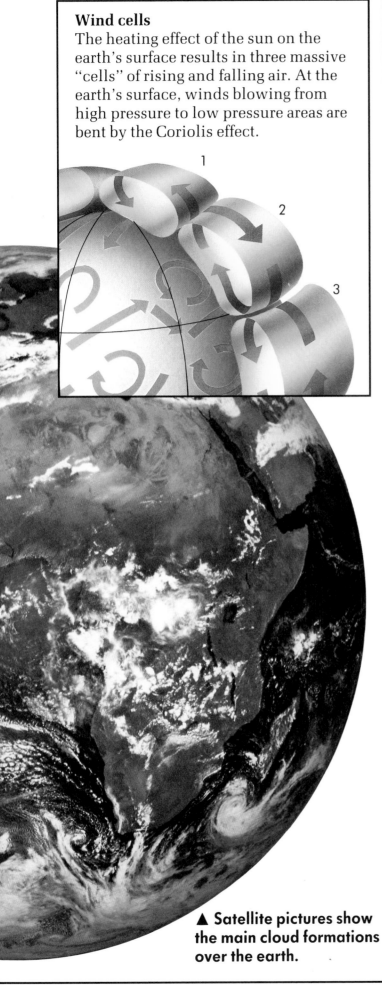

▲ **Satellite pictures show the main cloud formations over the earth.**

Clouds

Clouds are formed when air cools to a temperature at which it can no longer hold all its water as vapor. Water droplets are formed, which appear as clouds. The different types of clouds are shown below. Black, heavy cumulonimbus clouds often warn of a storm.

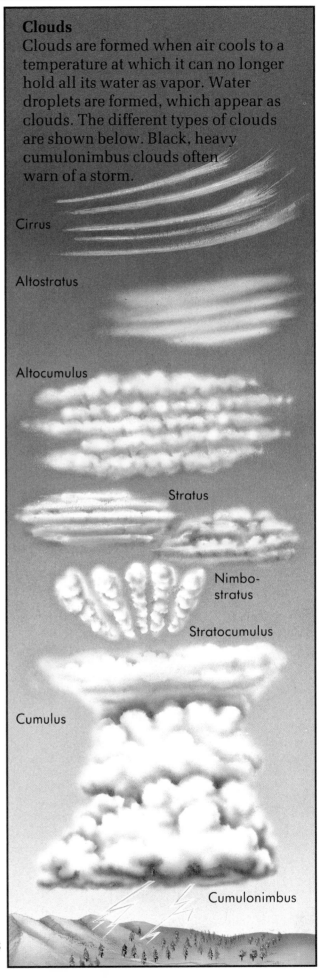

Cirrus

Altostratus

Altocumulus

Stratus

Nimbo-
stratus

Stratocumulus

Cumulus

Cumulonimbus

WHAT IS A HURRICANE?

A hurricane is a large, spinning wind system that develops over warm seas near the equator. These areas are known as the tropics. Technically, hurricanes are called tropical revolving storms, but they also have local names. They are called hurricanes when they occur over the Atlantic Ocean, typhoons in the Far East, and cyclones in the Indian Ocean. By definition, all are characterized by rotating winds that exceed speeds of 75 mph on the Beaufort wind scale.

The tropics are the hottest parts of the world, and experience the most extreme weather conditions. Air heated by the sun rises swiftly, which creates areas of very low pressure. As the warm air rises, it becomes loaded with moisture that condenses into massive thunderclouds. Cool air rushes in to fill the void that is left, but because of the constant turning of the earth on its axis, the air is bent inward and then spirals upward with great force. The swirling winds rotate faster and faster, forming a huge circle that can be up to 1,200 miles across.

▲ The typhoon that hit Manila in the Philippines in 1988 caused severe flooding. People were forced to cling to items like tires to survive.

► The shattered remains of Darwin in Australia after Cyclone Tracy hit the area on Christmas Day in 1974. Tracy's winds reached 150 mph and battered the city for over four hours. 48,000 inhabitants were evacuated and 8,000 homes destroyed.

Extreme conditions

A spectacular part of tropical storms is the long, low thunderclouds that can be seen rolling across this landscape. The tinges of gray-black at the edges of the clouds are the result of undercurrents of cold air that force the moisture in the warmer air above to condense very quickly. It is these clouds that bring the torrential downpours of rain that accompany most thunderstorms. Thunder and lightning can also occur.

A HURRICANE BEGINS

Hurricanes usually begin in the steamy, late summer in the tropics, when the seas are at their warmest. For a hurricane to develop, the sea surface must have a temperature of at least 78°F. When warm air rises from the seas and condenses into clouds, massive amounts of heat are released. The result of this mixture of heat and moisture is often a collection of thunderstorms, from which a tropical storm can develop.

The trigger for most Atlantic hurricanes is an easterly wave, a band of low pressure moving westward (see illustration), which might have begun as an African thunderstorm. Vigorous thunderstorms and high winds combine to create a cluster of thunderstorms which can become the seedling for a tropical storm. Typhoons in the Far East and cyclones in the Indian Ocean often develop from a thunderstorm in the equatorial trough (see below). During the hurricane season, the Coriolis effect of the earth's rotation starts the winds in the thunderstorm spinning in a circular motion.

At the center of the storm is a calm, often cloudless area called the eye, where there is no rain, and the winds are fairly light.

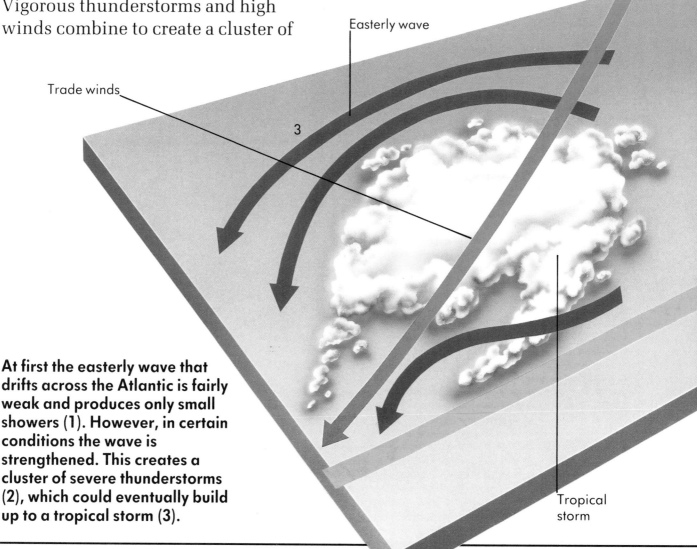

Trade winds

Easterly wave

3

Tropical storm

At first the easterly wave that drifts across the Atlantic is fairly weak and produces only small showers (1). However, in certain conditions the wave is strengthened. This creates a cluster of severe thunderstorms (2), which could eventually build up to a tropical storm (3).

Hurricane detection

The National Hurricane Center (shown right) was formed in 1959 in the United States. One of its aims is to investigate the amount of energy in a hurricane, and to understand the way in which the energy is distributed. Other objectives include studying how hurricanes work, and in what ways their impact could be controlled and reduced. Research is also being carried out concerning the forces that make hurricanes move from the spot where they first begin. Here, hurricane researchers are collecting and analyzing data that helps them to identify potential hurricanes.

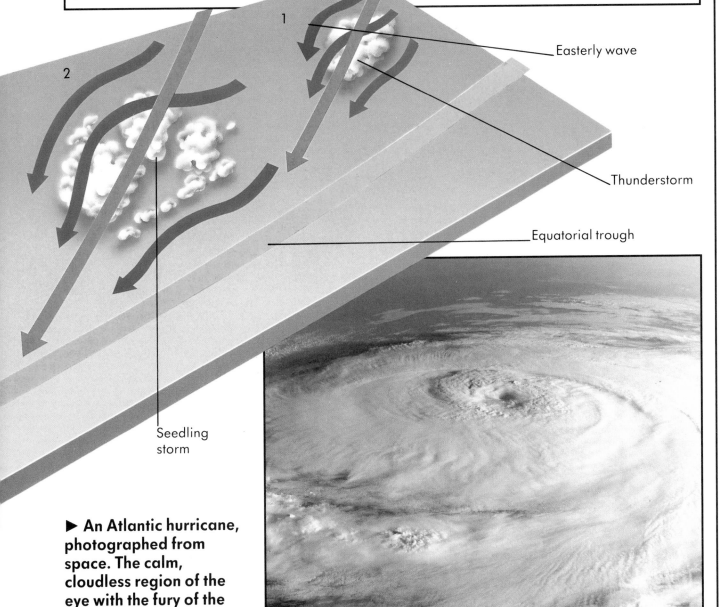

1

2

Easterly wave

Thunderstorm

Equatorial trough

Seedling storm

▶ **An Atlantic hurricane, photographed from space. The calm, cloudless region of the eye with the fury of the hurricane raging all around it is clearly visible.**

THE BUILDUP

As the hurricane builds up it begins to move. It is sustained by a steady flow of warm, moist air. The strongest winds and heaviest rains are found in the towering clouds which merge into a wall about 12-18 miles from the storm's center. Winds around the eye can reach speeds of up to 125 mph and a fully developed hurricane pumps out about two million tons of air per second. This results in more rain being released in a day than falls in a year on a city like New York.

The hurricane travels at speeds of between 10 and 30 mph. When it hits an area of cold sea or land, it enters a cold, inhospitable climate, where its supply of moist air is cut off. The eye quickly disappears and the storm begins to die down.

Yet it is when it hits the land that a hurricane, typhoon, or cyclone causes most damage. Ninety percent of victims are claimed when the storm first smashes ashore, bringing with it not only powerful winds, but huge waves called storm surges.

Clouds

The clouds are kept swirling around the eye by the strength of the wind. They spin around like a huge pinwheel.

◀ **The air in the eye is calm and smooth at most heights, and is much warmer than that of the surrounding clouds of the hurricane.**

88

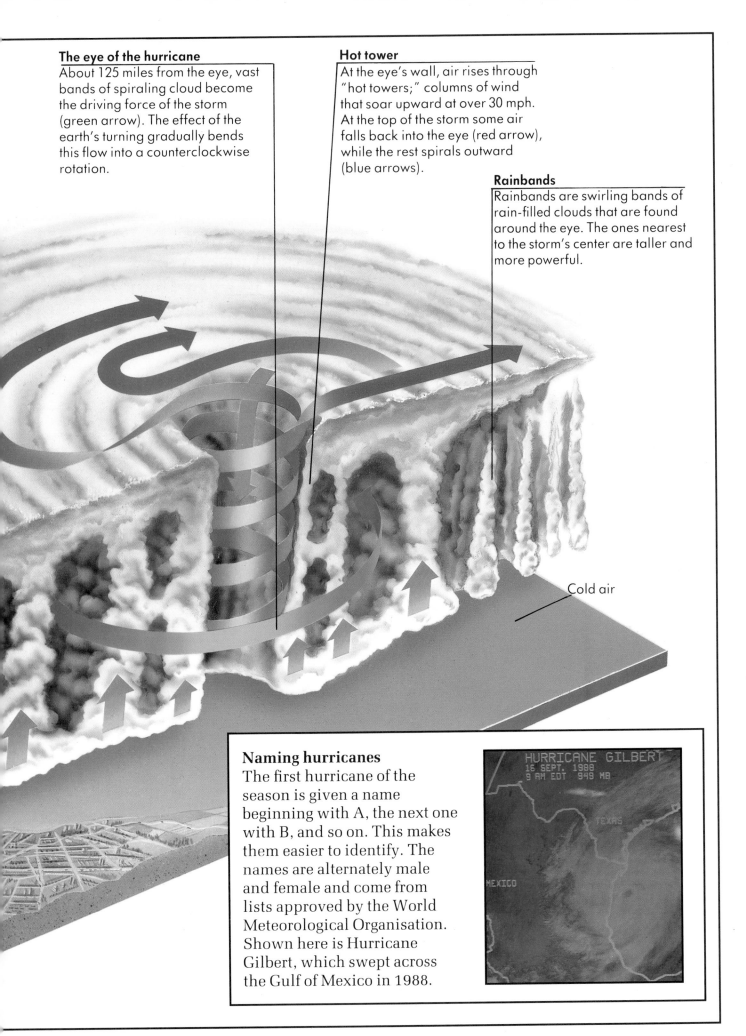

The eye of the hurricane
About 125 miles from the eye, vast bands of spiraling cloud become the driving force of the storm (green arrow). The effect of the earth's turning gradually bends this flow into a counterclockwise rotation.

Hot tower
At the eye's wall, air rises through "hot towers;" columns of wind that soar upward at over 30 mph. At the top of the storm some air falls back into the eye (red arrow), while the rest spirals outward (blue arrows).

Rainbands
Rainbands are swirling bands of rain-filled clouds that are found around the eye. The ones nearest to the storm's center are taller and more powerful.

Cold air

Naming hurricanes
The first hurricane of the season is given a name beginning with A, the next one with B, and so on. This makes them easier to identify. The names are alternately male and female and come from lists approved by the World Meteorological Organisation. Shown here is Hurricane Gilbert, which swept across the Gulf of Mexico in 1988.

HURRICANE GILBERT
16 SEPT. 1988
9 AM EDT 949 MB

TEXAS

MEXICO

THE STORM SURGE

The deadly companion of every tropical storm is the storm surge; the huge mounds of seawater that are whipped up by the powerful winds.

The first sign of a storm surge can occur nearly a week before the actual hurricane, typhoon, or cyclone. Winds move outward much faster than the storm itself and whip up the sea into waves up to 5 ft high along the coastline. When the storm is about 110 miles from land, huge waves driven by its winds begin to crash ashore. The deafening roar of the surf can be heard miles inland. This is followed by the most deadly and destructive element of the surge as the huge bulge of water that forms beneath the storm's eye smashes ashore.

The effects of such storm surges are far-reaching. Low-lying coastal areas can be devastated by the severe floods that result, and many lives and homes are often lost. In the Far East, typhoons build up in the western Pacific Ocean and batter Japan and the Asian mainland. Cyclones that begin in the Indian Ocean can veer south toward East Africa.

Storm surges

A storm surge builds up out at sea as a tropical storm races in toward the shore. The sea level rises above the height of protective sand dunes on the shore. As the sea rushes in, it flattens the dunes and swamps the land behind them. This town will be flooded by the storm surge.

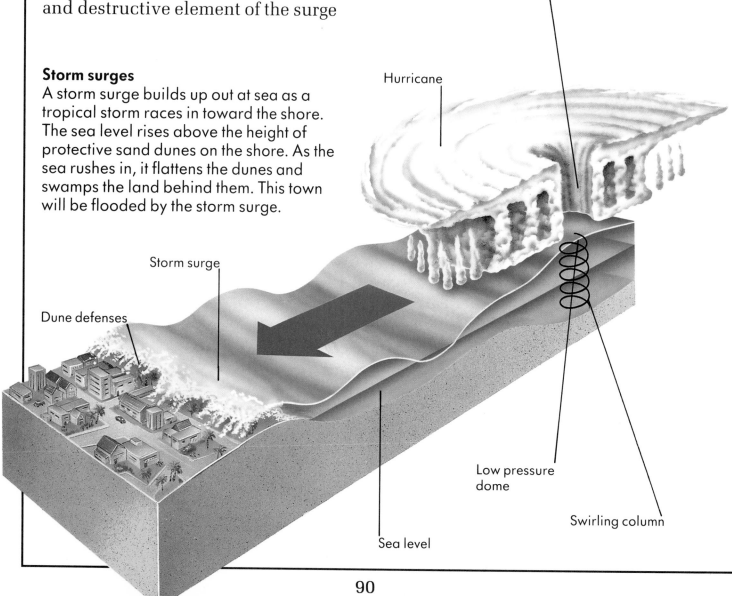

Hurricane's eye

Hurricane

Storm surge

Dune defenses

Low pressure dome

Swirling column

Sea level

Into the storm

The unpredictability of tropical storms and the speed with which they can suddenly change course have caught the crews of many ships at sea unawares.

Equipped to deal with such emergencies are tug boats like the "Abeille-Languedoc" (shown right), which often have to undertake rescue missions arising from storms at sea.

Sea storms in history

For ships at sea, no storm poses a greater threat than a fully-developed hurricane or winds of hurricane force. Although sailing ships were built to withstand gales and storms, the winds and mountainous seas created by such extreme weather phenomena often caused great damage. In this illustration, desperate sailors are seen trying to stay afloat as their ships sink in the maelstrom of the English Channel. This storm was one of the worst in England's history. It struck in November 1703 and its hurricane-force winds claimed about 8,000 lives and destroyed more than 14,000 homes.

▲ A U.S. destroyer caught in the enormous waves formed by a typhoon in December, 1944. The storm was so severe that the captain described the waves as being "like vertical mountains."

A FREAK ON LAND

In many ways, a tornado resembles a miniature hurricane. However, tornadoes are far more powerful than hurricanes. This is because their fearsome energy is concentrated into a violently spinning column of air less than one mile across.

Unlike hurricanes, tornadoes tend to form over the land. Central North America experiences more tornadoes than anywhere else in the world. They usually occur during cloudy, stormy weather and descend from a severe thunderstorm as a rapidly spinning white funnel of cloud. Dust and soil are drawn up into the funnel in a spiral that can be seen hurtling across the landscape. A screaming roar pierces the ears and scythelike winds cut through even the strongest of buildings. Cars, camper vans, and even airplanes have been picked up, carried away, and then dropped and smashed like toys.

When it touches the ground the tornado quickly turns gray with dust and develops ragged edges. It becomes weaker, can no longer suck up the air in its path, and gradually dies out.

The ultimate storm

Tornadoes are the strongest winds in the world and can often cause total destruction of the area they hit. As the tornado's funnel tightens, the winds begin to spin faster and faster. The rotating winds pick up dust and debris, and the tornado is surrounded by an envelope of dust. Inside the dust envelope, the strongest winds can be found rotating at speeds of up to 180 mph around a calm, central eye of low pressure. This is known as the funnel cloud. Because the tornado's lowest pressure is near the ground, air that is sucked up into the funnel at first gains speed as it spirals around the eye. The air gradually slows down and spreads out as it reaches the heavy cumulonimbus clouds that are found at the top of the tornado.

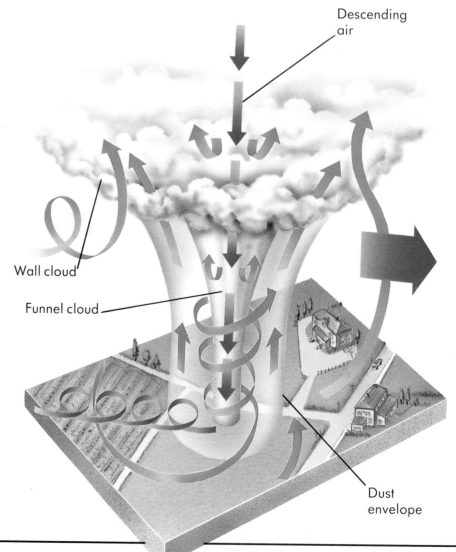

Descending air

Wall cloud

Funnel cloud

Dust envelope

A waterspout is a funnel of air that extends down from a cloud over the sea. In the same way as a tornado sucks up soil and debris, the waterspout sucks up great quantities of water. This gives the funnel its dark color (right). Waterspouts are much weaker than tornadoes and their winds rarely exceed speeds of 50 mph. They only usually last for about 15 minutes and occur mainly over shallow coastal waters.

THE DAMAGE

For anyone caught in a hurricane, the experience is a terrifying one. Fierce, whirling winds rip across the countryside, overturning cars and heavy trucks. Trees are ripped from the ground, and whole buildings can be lifted from their foundations.

Some of the worst disasters occur near coastal areas, where stormy seas contribute to the havoc that is wreaked. In 1938, one of the most powerful hurricanes in history swept through Long Island, New York. In just seven hours, the storm killed at least 600 people and destroyed the homes of over 60,000. The total damage was estimated at the enormous sum of one-third of one billion dollars. The storm destroyed 26,000 cars and 29,000 miles of electric, telegraph, and telephone wires and flooded thousands of acres of land.

One coastal area on the island was so badly hit by the hurricane that 200 homes there were completely swept away. Rescue workers searching for missing people had to use maps from telephone companies to identify the sites on which the houses once stood.

▲ The storm surge that hit Bangladesh's low-lying deltas in 1991 claimed hundreds of thousands of lives.

◀▼ When Hurricane Hugo hit Puerto Rico in 1989, 15 people were killed and 50,000 left homeless. Roofs were blown off, buildings demolished, and low-lying areas flooded by the rains and high waves.

PLOTTING THE PATH

No one can do anything to prevent a hurricane. The only thing weather forecasters can do is to try and plot the hurricane's path. People living in the area can then be warned and evacuated if necessary.

Weather stations all over the world exchange information about winds, rainfall, cloud, temperature, and air pressure. Satellites in space circle Earth and take photographs of the atmosphere from above, which can be used to show how clouds are forming.

At the first signs that a tropical storm is building up, information can be fed into computers to try to predict its course. First a band of low pressure develops over tropical seas

in an area that has spawned tropical storms in the past. For example, storms near the west coast of Africa have led to violent hurricanes and storm surges that later hit the islands of the Caribbean. In 1985, hurricane experts in the United States spotted a storm of this type and plotted its course as it developed into Hurricane Gloria. One million people had to be evacuated from their homes on the east coast of the United States.

▼ **The colors on infrared pictures of tropical storms help meteorologists to measure temperature and rainfall in different parts of the hurricane, and to estimate the storm's strength and course.**

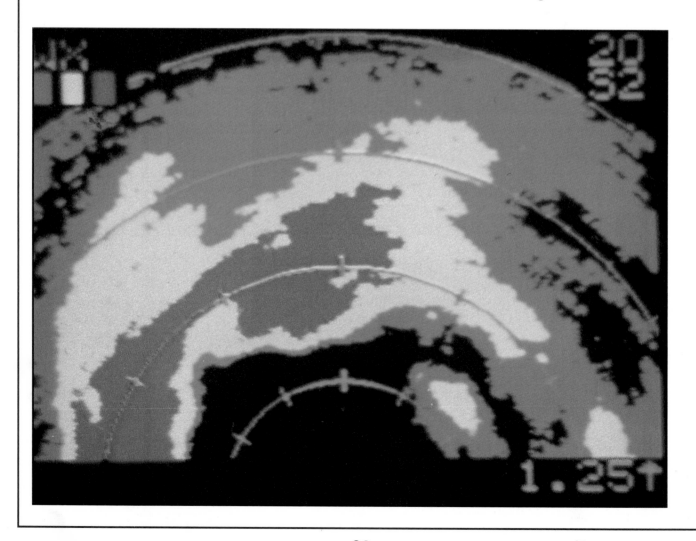

▶ Scientists at Colorado's Environmental Research Laboratories are combining sophisticated new instruments with computer technology to create a new "minute by minute" weather warning system. The system uses special radar devices, called profilers, that are directed toward the sky. Sophisticated computer equipment and other monitoring systems are also used. In this way, changes in the atmosphere can be quickly detected, and storms can be recognized even as they are forming. The storm's movement is then charted on screens (shown right).

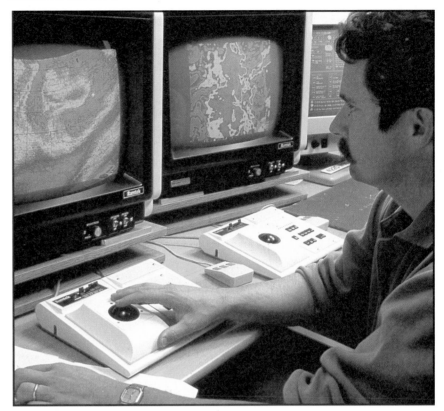

▼ Satellites in space play a major role in helping scientists to investigate and understand the changes in climate that lead to extreme weather conditions like tropical storms. The satellites map ocean waves, currents and tides, as well as the sea's surface temperatures and winds around the world.

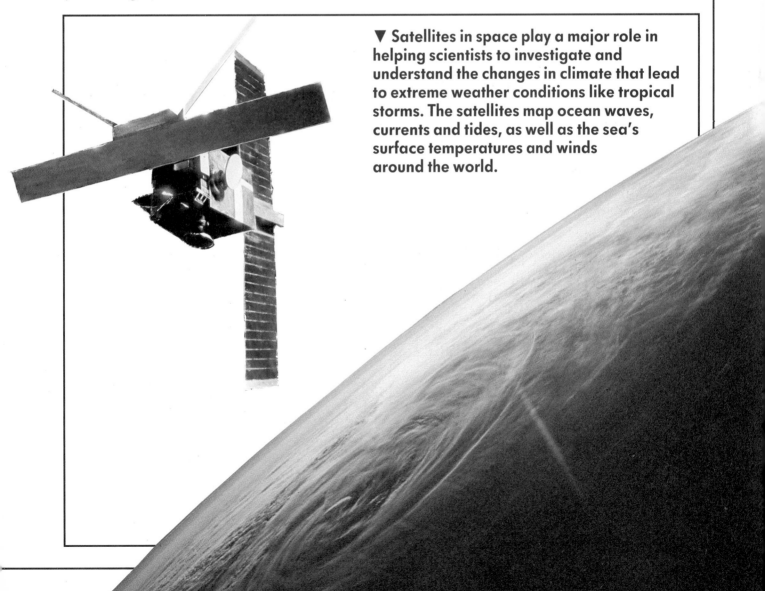

LIVING WITH THE THREAT

The threat of hurricanes is an ever-present one. Even if precautions are taken, they can still cause misery and devastation.

However, some countries are too poor to take precautions, and unfortunately, it is often these areas that are hit most severely by tropical storms. Bangladesh is in southern Asia. It is one of the world's poorest countries, and about 100 million people eke out a living by farming the fertile mud flats at the mouth of the Ganges River. This area is often hit by violent cyclones, such as the one that swept through the area in April 1991. Thousands of people have been killed as massive storm surges swept over them and their flimsy homes. Those who do survive have no homes and no food or clean water. In such conditions diseases such as cholera quickly spread, making the death toll even higher.

Building defenses

Seawalls are the best protection for towns near the sea. Some walls have tops that curve outward so that the waves are turned back on themselves as they break against them. Others have teeth or ridges that are designed to break up the wave and reduce its impact. When floods do occur, pumping stations are needed to get rid of the water quickly. Shutters or boards can be used to protect windows from smashing. The window in the picture below has been covered with strips of tape to stop it from shattering.

Clearing up the mess

The damage caused by a hurricane can take months or even years to repair. People are often forced to salvage what little they have left from their flooded or wrecked homes (below right). Roads have to be cleared and fallen debris removed (below). Electricity and phone lines have to be repaired. Emergency food and water supplies might have to be brought in to the affected area. After Hurricane Hugo struck Puerto Rico, power plants there were so badly damaged that three-quarters of the homes in the area were without power. Oil storage tanks were also badly damaged (photo bottom).

ARE WE CAUSING MORE?

Hurricanes are sustained by warm, moist air. The countries of northern Europe have a fairly cool climate. So why have they been hit by hurricanes in recent years?

One theory is that global warming is having some effect. As the planet heats up, more parts of the world are developing the kind of climate that is ideal for tropical storms.

The gases in the earth's atmosphere act like the glass of a greenhouse, trapping enough heat from the sun to keep the planet warm enough for life. This is known as the "Greenhouse Effect." One of the main greenhouse gases is carbon dioxide. Other greenhouse gases are methane, water vapor, and chlorofluorocarbons (CFCs). The only way we can prevent global warming is by controlling the amounts of these gases that are released into the atmosphere.

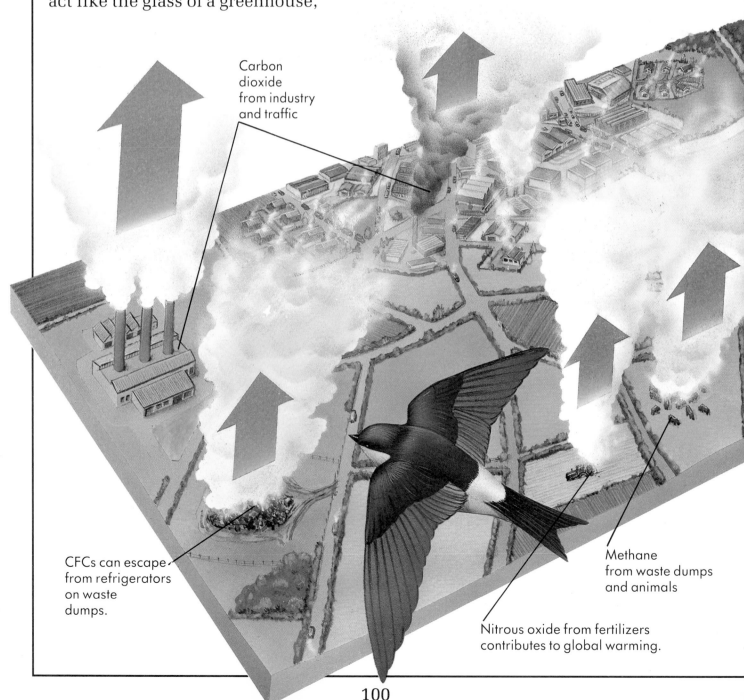

Carbon dioxide from industry and traffic

CFCs can escape from refrigerators on waste dumps.

Methane from waste dumps and animals

Nitrous oxide from fertilizers contributes to global warming.

The Greenhouse Effect

The atmosphere allows sunlight through to heat the earth, but traps some of the heat that radiates back toward space. This is rather like the way the glass in a greenhouse works, and so is called the Greenhouse Effect. The gases that prevent some of the heat from escaping into space are known as greenhouse gases. They help to maintain the right temperatures on Earth for life. If too many greenhouse gases are present however, too much warmth is trapped, which could make global temperatures rise.

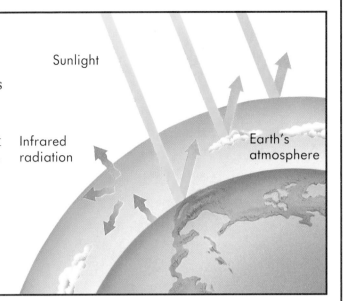

Sunlight

Infrared radiation

Earth's atmosphere

Water vapor

► Carbon dioxide occurs naturally in the atmosphere, but is also produced by burning fuels in factories and power plants, and is emitted in traffic exhaust fumes. Plants absorb carbon dioxide, but clearing large areas of rain forests means there are fewer plants to do this. Levels of carbon dioxide in the atmosphere therefore increase.

WHAT CAN WE DO?

In the rich, industrialized countries, meteorologists are working on ways of improving information and warning systems, and of pinpointing danger zones. However, even when sophisticated equipment is used, and information is processed by computer, hurricanes can still take people by surprise. If the storm suddenly changes course, the evacuation of an area might not be possible. Precautions should therefore be taken to reduce the impact of the hurricane, typhoon, or cyclone and to offer protection for people in its path.

In low-lying areas, special shelters can be built for this purpose. Bangladesh has 63 cyclone shelters. They are raised 13 feet from the ground and built to withstand even greater forces than those experienced during the latest cyclone. Each shelter can hold up to 1,500 people, but about 350,000 people made use of them during the latest disaster.

Preventing global warming

There are several ways to reduce the amount of harmful greenhouse gases currently being pumped into the atmosphere. For example, to reduce carbon dioxide levels, we must start by burning less fossil fuels, both in industry (below) and at home. This can be done by using alternative sources of energy, like wind, water, and solar power, which do not release carbon dioxide into the atmosphere. Homes and factories can be made more efficient so that they use less energy. And forests can be replanted to stop carbon dioxide building up in the atmosphere.

► Teams of hurricane experts around the world gather information about changes in the weather. Warnings and progress reports can be issued every few hours via radio and television once a possible storm has been identified.

▼ Scientists use planes like the one shown below to journey into the eye of a hurricane. The plane's probe, which is located in front of the nose, gives instant information on the pressure and humidity inside the hurricane, thereby enabling scientists to calculate its strength.

FACTFILE: *Hurricanes & Typhoons*

The cyclones that hit Bangladesh

Bangladesh has been the victim of many cyclones which cause flooding of the Ganges delta. In 1970, a tropical cyclone claimed 500,000 lives there. Thousands died in 1985 when a massive wall of water swept over the mud flats where people lived and farmed the land.

In April 1991, a devastating cyclone raced into the Bay of Bengal at 140 mph, and waves nearly 23 feet high flooded many communities on the coast. It is thought that 250,000 people may have been killed, some of them on fishing boats and others in flimsy houses made of mud and straw. This is the worst cyclone to hit Bangladesh this century, with stronger winds than the 1970 storm. Warnings were given, but many people did not have radios or television so they did not hear them. Others did not believe the cyclone would hit them because there had been several false alarms. About 10 million people were left homeless. They had no food and only muddy, salty water to drink. Millions more people may die from starvation and diseases such as cholera.

Tropical storms in history

1737 Cyclone storm surge killed 300,000 people in the Calcutta area of India.
1899 300 people killed in Bathurst, Queensland by a 50 ft storm surge, formed as a result of cyclone winds.
1900 A hurricane and storm surge hit Galveston, Texas, causing about 6,000 deaths.
1945 2,000 people killed by a typhoon in Japan – just 42 days after the devastation of Hiroshima by a nuclear bomb.
1953 307 people killed by hurricane force winds. A storm surge was created which washed over the east coast of England. The same surge claimed over 1,800 lives in Holland.
1963 Hurricane Flora killed 5,000 people on the island of Haiti in the Caribbean.
1969 Hurricane Camille caused destruction from Louisiana to Virginia killing 250 people.
1970 Hurricane Celia killed 11 people on the Texas coast.
500,000 were killed by a cyclone in Bangladesh.
1972 122 people from Florida to New York were killed by floods during Hurricane Agnes.
1974 About 8,000 people were killed by Hurricane Fifi in Honduras, Central America.
1974 Cyclone Tracy flattened the city of Darwin in Australia.
1976 Hurricane Liza killed 400 people in Mexico.
1979 Hurricane David hit Puerto Rico and the southeast coast of the United States, causing 4,000 deaths.
1980 Hurricane Allen hit the Caribbean Islands, killing 272 people.
1983 Hurricane Alicia killed 21 people in Galveston, Texas.

Tornado terrors

The United States has more than 850 tornadoes a year. Most tornadoes happen between April and October. The most disastrous in terms of lives lost was in the midwestern states in 1925, when 689 people were killed. But others have had devastating consequences too. In April 1979, a tornado struck the city of Wichita Falls in Texas. By the time it had passed, the city looked as though it had been bombed: 20,000 people were left homeless and 46 were killed. Sometimes several tornadoes start at once. In 1974, 148 tornadoes killed 315 people in 13 states over a period of two days. In April 1991, a series of tornadoes ripped through the states of Kansas and Oklahoma, flattening hundreds of homes and destroying a trailer park containing 400 mobile homes. Hundreds of people were injured and more than 30 people were killed.

The highest storm surge

The highest storm surge was in 1969 during Hurricane Camille, when a wave 25 feet high flooded the coast at Pass Christian, Mississippi.

Chapter Five

TIDAL WAVES
AND FLOODING

CONTENTS

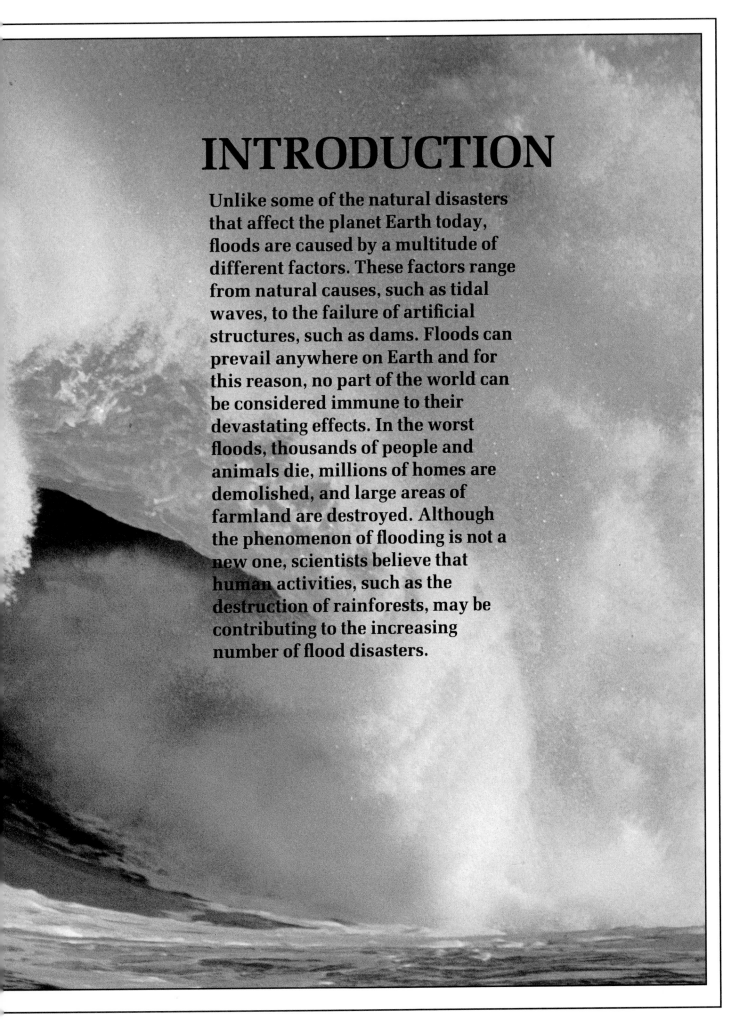

INTRODUCTION

Unlike some of the natural disasters that affect the planet Earth today, floods are caused by a multitude of different factors. These factors range from natural causes, such as tidal waves, to the failure of artificial structures, such as dams. Floods can prevail anywhere on Earth and for this reason, no part of the world can be considered immune to their devastating effects. In the worst floods, thousands of people and animals die, millions of homes are demolished, and large areas of farmland are destroyed. Although the phenomenon of flooding is not a new one, scientists believe that human activities, such as the destruction of rainforests, may be contributing to the increasing number of flood disasters.

WHAT ARE FLOODS?

Floods are the waters which cover an area of land that is normally dry. They have affected almost every corner of the earth at some time or another, but those which cause the greatest amount of damage are the result of extreme weather conditions.

Tropical storms, which are called typhoons, hurricanes, or cyclones in different parts of the world, whip up the winds over the oceans and create huge waves. These waves, known as storm surges, race toward the shore and crash onto the coastline. The country of Bangladesh has suffered serious flooding on many occasions, as cyclones in the Bay of Bengal send huge sea waves crashing over the low-lying coastal areas. Other enormous waves which produce severe flooding are the so-called tidal waves, or *tsunamis*, which result from earthquakes or volcanic eruptions.

The millions of tons of rock, soil, and mud unleashed during a landslide can block a river valley or dam, causing water levels to rise dramatically. Flooding can also follow a seiche, the violent movement of lake waters following an earthquake. The most frequent cause, however, is when heavy rains and melting snow and ice make inland rivers and dams burst. This problem is made worse in areas where large numbers of trees have been cleared. Stripped of their vegetation, the hillsides cannot hold the excess water, which runs off and causes flooding in lowland areas.

◄ During powerful storms, strong winds whip up high waves that pound down on the coastline. Sea defenses are often smashed to pieces, causing serious flooding in areas along the coast and extensive damage to property.

► Sudden, violent bursts of water surging down narrow mountain valleys or dry river beds are called flash floods. These raging torrents of water, such as the one shown right at El Oued in Algeria, can flood an area for just a few hours, or even minutes, before subsiding.

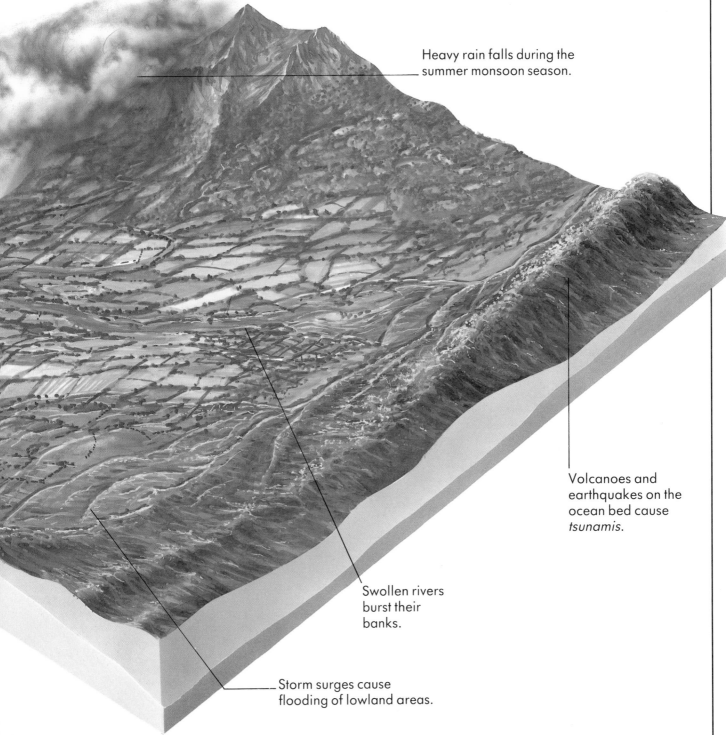

Heavy rain falls during the summer monsoon season.

Volcanoes and earthquakes on the ocean bed cause *tsunamis*.

Swollen rivers burst their banks.

Storm surges cause flooding of lowland areas.

WHAT IS A TIDAL WAVE?

When an earthquake occurs on the ocean floor, it releases huge amounts of energy in shock waves. These waves travel outward in ripplelike movements called seismic waves. They spread out from the center, or focus, of the earthquake, causing the seabed to jolt and shift. These movements of the seabed create enormous waves which can pass through open seas at speeds of between 400 and 500 miles per hour, depending on the depth of the sea. The waves are called *tsunamis*, after the Japanese word for "storm waves." They are sometimes referred to as "tidal waves," although they have nothing to do with tides.

In deep waters, *tsunamis* are low and wide, often less than three feet high and with as much as 95 miles between the crest of one wave and the next one. Yet, when the waves reach shallower water, they become more deadly as they rear up to heights of 100 feet or more, and crash inland, causing widespread devastation.

Using special equipment, scientists can predict *tsunamis* in some parts of the world. The Tsunami Warning System in Hawaii monitors seismic activity in the Pacific region.

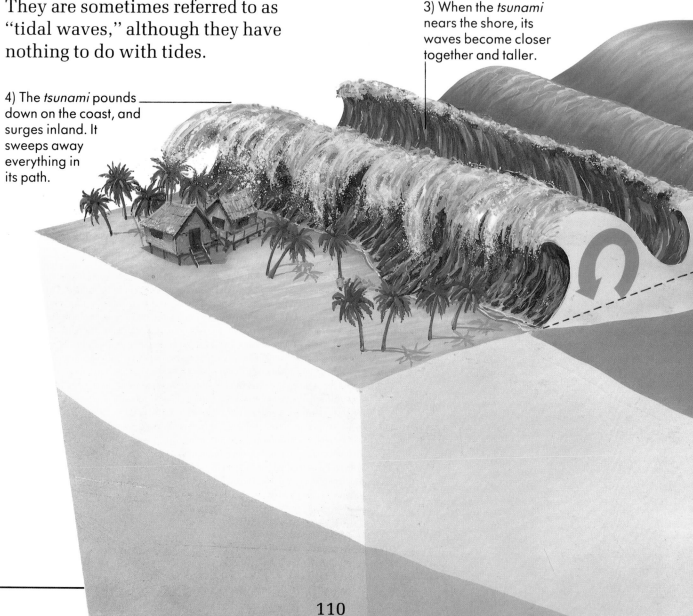

3) When the *tsunami* nears the shore, its waves become closer together and taller.

4) The *tsunami* pounds _____ down on the coast, and surges inland. It sweeps away everything in its path.

Volcanic causes

Tsunamis can also be caused when an underwater volcano or a volcanic island erupts. After the volcanic island of Krakatau exploded in 1883, a *tsunami* 115 feet high smashed into the islands of Java and Sumatra, killing 36,000 people. Ninety percent of all recorded *tsunamis* have been in the Pacific Ocean, where there are over 10,000 volcanoes.

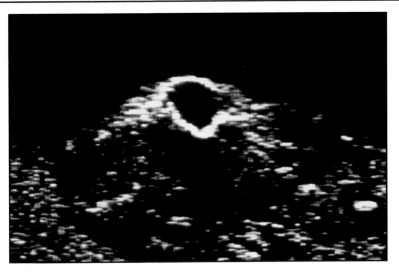

2) The seismic waves make the seafloor jolt, which creates huge sea waves.

1) When an earthquake occurs below the ocean floor, part of the seabed is forced upward.

A *tsunami* may strike without warning, often on a calm day. The earthquake which unleashed it probably occurred far away, so the shock waves would not be felt on land. The largest recorded *tsunami* (280 ft. high) surged past the Japanese island of Ishigaki in 1971.

THE WORLD'S WATER

The world's water supply is constantly circulating around the earth in a process known as the water, or hydrological, cycle. Heat from the sun's rays causes some of the water in the world's oceans, lakes, rivers, and streams to evaporate and turn into water vapor. This vapor rises up into the air and condenses to form clouds. The water droplets in the clouds fall back down to Earth as rain or snow, most of which falls into the oceans. About one-tenth falls into streams and rivers on the land, and is eventually carried back to the oceans.

This natural cycle of water is altered in a number of ways. Storm rains and sudden climatic changes, such as a rise in temperature, result in excess quantities of water which cannot be absorbed by the soil, vegetation, or atmosphere, or channeled in the normal way.

River

Evaporation
Water vapor rises up into the air from oceans, rivers, and lakes, cools and forms clouds.

Ocean

About 98 percent of the water in the water cycle comes from oceans, rivers, lakes, and streams. The remaining 2 percent comes from the water vapor given off by plants, mostly through their leaves. This process is called transpiration.

Transpiration

112

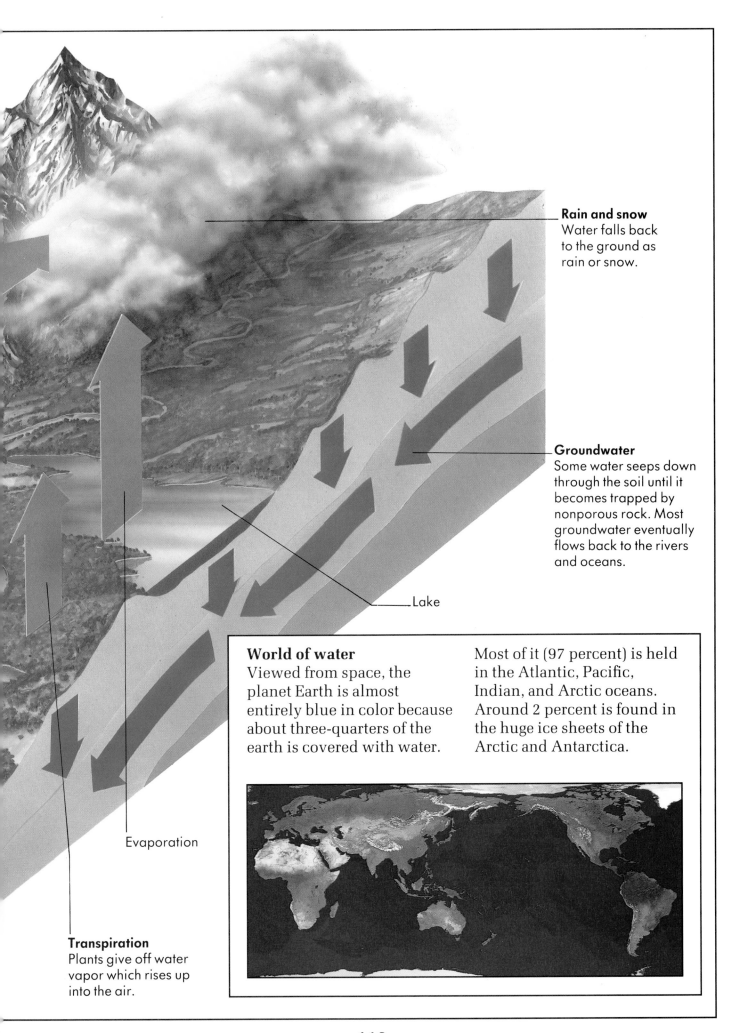

Rain and snow
Water falls back to the ground as rain or snow.

Groundwater
Some water seeps down through the soil until it becomes trapped by nonporous rock. Most groundwater eventually flows back to the rivers and oceans.

Lake

World of water
Viewed from space, the planet Earth is almost entirely blue in color because about three-quarters of the earth is covered with water.

Most of it (97 percent) is held in the Atlantic, Pacific, Indian, and Arctic oceans. Around 2 percent is found in the huge ice sheets of the Arctic and Antarctica.

Evaporation

Transpiration
Plants give off water vapor which rises up into the air.

THE AFTEREFFECTS

In the aftermath of a severe flood, thousands of people and animals are drowned, and whole villages are demolished. Tens of thousands of square miles of farmland are ruined as the crops and fertile soil are washed away and replaced by thick mud.

Floods also cause massive destruction of roads, bridges, railroad lines, and water and power supplies. Rescue workers have difficulty in bringing food and medicines to the many people trapped by the flood waters. Broken sewers and the lack of clean water can lead to the rapid spread of diseases like cholera.

In November 1991, tropical storm Thelma struck the island of Leyte in the Philippines, causing the worst floods there in seven years. Over 2,500 people died, thousands more were reported missing and an estimated 50,000 were left homeless.

◀▲ Flooding in the Philippines in November 1991 left the streets of Ormoc, on Leyte Island, filled with mud, water, dead bodies, and piles of debris.

▶ The summer monsoon season in India lasts for up to three months each year. Many cities and towns are flooded for weeks on end. The city of Cherrapunji receives an average of 240 inches of rain each year. This is one of the world's highest annual rainfall totals.

THE FLOODED COAST

Many coastlines suffer from serious flooding, either due to unusually high tides or because the land lies below sea level. In January 1953, winds of over 115 mph combined with the high tide to produce storm surges. Vast areas of fertile land along the North Sea coastline of several countries were flooded. Sea levels reached 16 feet above normal, and over 1,800 people were killed.

Most of the population of Bangladesh live on the lowlands of the Ganges Delta on the Bay of Bengal. Despite the high risk of flooding on the tidal lands there, the fertile soil offers the poor of Bangladesh a place to build their homes and to farm. In 1970 the world's greatest sea flood from a tropical cyclone in the area, left half a million people dead.

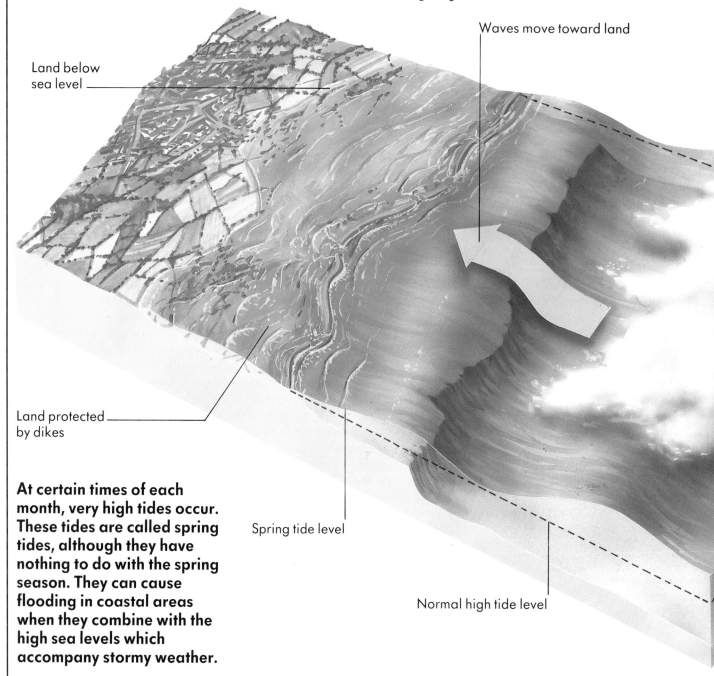

Waves move toward land

Land below sea level

Land protected by dikes

Spring tide level

Normal high tide level

At certain times of each month, very high tides occur. These tides are called spring tides, although they have nothing to do with the spring season. They can cause flooding in coastal areas when they combine with the high sea levels which accompany stormy weather.

The Netherlands

Much of the land along the coast of The Netherlands lies below sea level and is known as the polders. Prins Alexander polder, the lowest in the country, lies nearly 23 feet below sea level. To protect the polders from flooding, huge protective walls called dikes have been built along the coast. A 20-mile dike called the Afluitsdijk separates the North Sea from a huge freshwater lake, the Ijsselmeer (right).

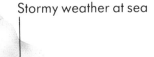

Stormy weather at sea

► **Flooding in Bangladesh after a cyclone in 1991 killed over 250,000 people. Extensive damage to the surrounding area (right) left over 10 million people homeless.**

CITIES UNDER THREAT

In the developing world, many cities are built in areas that are prone to regular coastal flooding. In Guayaquil in Ecuador, more than half the population lives in shanty dwellings which suffer from regular sea flooding, as well as flooding from the nearby Guayas River. Another city built on tidal land is Jakarta in Indonesia, where many of the urban poor build their flimsy, makeshift houses on low-lying land.

Large areas of London, including the underground train system and the docks, are built at or below sea level. In January 1953, the River Thames rose by over 3 feet above the spring tide level, breaking through its protective walls, which are known as embankments, in several places. To avoid the risk of future floods, a tidal flood defense system called the Thames Barrier has been built across the river at Woolwich. The barrier, which was opened in 1984, consists of a wall of 10 steel gates. These gates can be closed to prevent flood waters surging upstream.

▶ **The gates of the Thames Barrier sit on the river bed in the open position. When the water level rises, they are rotated by large wheellike structures so that they are in a vertical position and close the openings between the piers, sealing off the river beyond.**

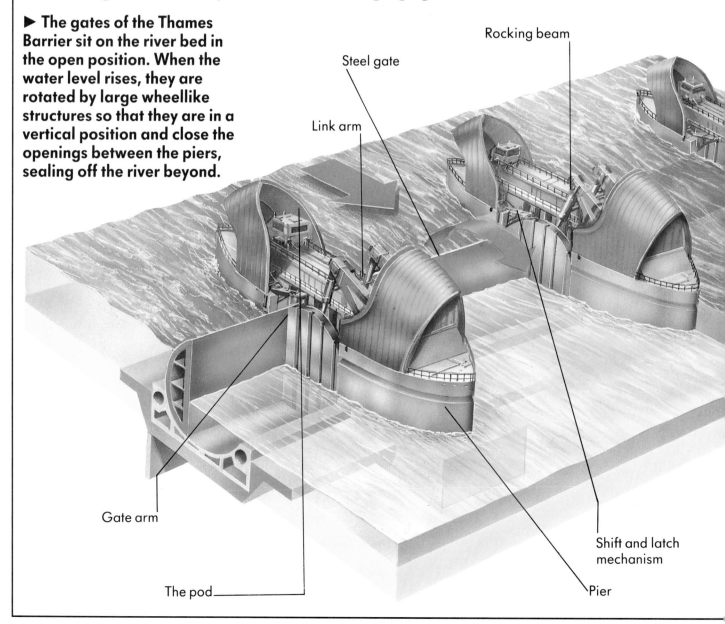

Rocking beam

Steel gate

Link arm

Gate arm

The pod

Shift and latch mechanism

Pier

118

Florence, 1966

In 1966, the River Arno in Italy broke its banks, covering the low-lying districts of Florence in about 20 feet of mud and water. The flood waters surged through the streets so rapidly that thousands of people were stranded on the top floors of their homes. Many priceless art treasures were destroyed or damaged.

▶ The vast St. Petersburg Dike (right) in the Soviet Union is intended to protect the city of St. Petersburg from frequent flooding by the River Neva. However, after objections from environmentalists, work on the dike project was halted in the fall of 1990.

RIVER FLOODS

Rivers are responsible for more floods than lakes or seas. Many rivers overflow their banks once or twice each year, often during the spring months. One reason why a river floods is because large amounts of ice and snow on nearby hills and mountains suddenly melt. The frozen ground cannot soak up the extra water, and the rapid thaw gives rise to severe flooding. Another reason is too much rainfall within a short period of time. Asian rivers often flood after the heavy rains of the monsoon season. The calm river waters swell with the extra water, and turn into a raging muddy torrent.

For centuries, snow melts from the Alps have caused the River Po to flood through Northern Italy. The nutrients brought down in the flood waters from the mountains have made this area extremely fertile. However, these flood waters are also making the city of Venice sink further below the water level each year.

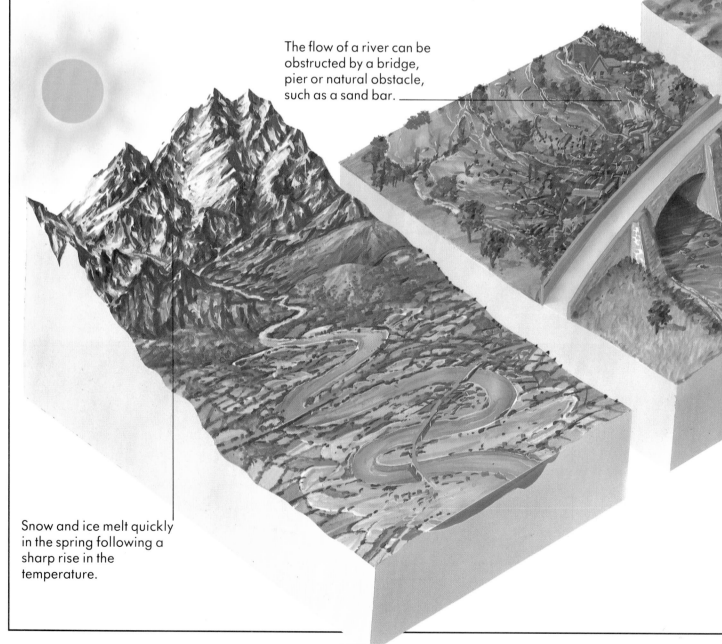

The flow of a river can be obstructed by a bridge, pier or natural obstacle, such as a sand bar.

Snow and ice melt quickly in the spring following a sharp rise in the temperature.

A river channel is a hollowed-out passageway made by flowing water. The size and position of the channel change as the flow of water erodes one part of the bank, and builds up another.

Torrential rain quickly soaks into the land until the soil cannot hold any more water.

Monsoon winds bring very heavy rains to southern Asia between May and October.

▶ In July 1976, over 12 inches of rain fell in the Big Thompson River valley in the Rocky Mountains in just four and a half hours. The flood waters tore apart the local interstate highway, tossing into the air huge chunks of tarmac. Houses, bridges, camping vehicles, and people were swept away by the raging torrent of water.

FLOODS IN HISTORY

Throughout history, floods have had a major impact on people and their surroundings. One of the most famous flood legends is the story of Noah and his Ark from the Old Testament. After 40 days of heavy rains, the whole earth was flooded. So Noah and his wife took refuge, together with dozens of different animals, in a huge wooden boat until the waters subsided.

In Greek literature, the story about the flood of Deucalion is very similar to that of Noah's Ark. Deucalion was the father of Hellen, ancestor of the Hellenic race. Legend has it that Zeus, king of the Greek gods, was so disgusted with the behavior of mankind that he created a flood. Deucalion, however, had built a boat which he and his wife drifted in during the nine days of the flood.

According to the North American Indians, the spring floods were caused by a mouse chewing a hole in a bag that contained the sun's rays. The heat escaped through the hole and melted the winter snows.

The River Arno in Italy regularly floods the area around the city of Florence. The first recorded flood there dates back to the 2nd century A.D.

◄ The carving on this 12th-century altar in an Austrian convent depicts the dove returning to Noah's ark. In the story of Noah, flood waters were said to have covered the whole earth. It is believed that the flood occurred around 3,200 B.C. In 1929, archaeologists discovered evidence of a major flood by the Euphrates River in Mesopotamia (modern Iraq). The extent of the flood was so great that some historians believe it may have been the origin of the Noah's flood story.

▼ When the Yangtze River in China broke its banks in 1931, the river's waters rose some 100 feet above their normal level. They flooded the surrounding plains where almost half of the country's principal food crop, rice, is grown. The city of Hankou (below) was one of those affected by the flood waters. Over 3.5 million people died, either from drowning or from famine.

Da Vinci's plans to stop flooding
Leonardo da Vinci was a great engineer, architect, and artist who lived in Italy in the 16th century. He drew up plans for a flood-control system on the River Arno. His designs included a large basin to store excess water, a canal and floodgates to bring the river under control, all of which were later rejected.

ARE WE CAUSING MORE?

In many areas of the world, more and more land is being cleared of trees and other vegetation. This deforestation provides much needed farmland on which to produce food for the world's growing population. But it also causes soil erosion, with a greater risk of lowland flooding. Severe flooding in the Philippines in 1991 was blamed on tree-felling activities in the region.

Deforestation, together with the burning of fossil fuels and trees, increases the amount of carbon dioxide in the atmosphere. Carbon dioxide is a "greenhouse gas," which means that it helps to trap enough heat close to the earth's surface for life to survive. However, if the amount of greenhouse gases in the atmosphere increases because of

pollution or the burning of trees, temperatures around the world could rise. Increases of between 2.5 and 4.5 degrees Fahrenheit could lead to climatic changes.

Power plants and factories burn fossil fuels that produce greenhouse gases.

Rising sea levels
Scientists are worried that the slow but steady increase in the world's temperatures might make the world's ice sheets and glaciers begin to melt, raising sea levels across the world. At present, they estimate that the sea level is rising by about 0.3 inches each year. If this trend were to continue, low-lying countries could be left permanently under water.

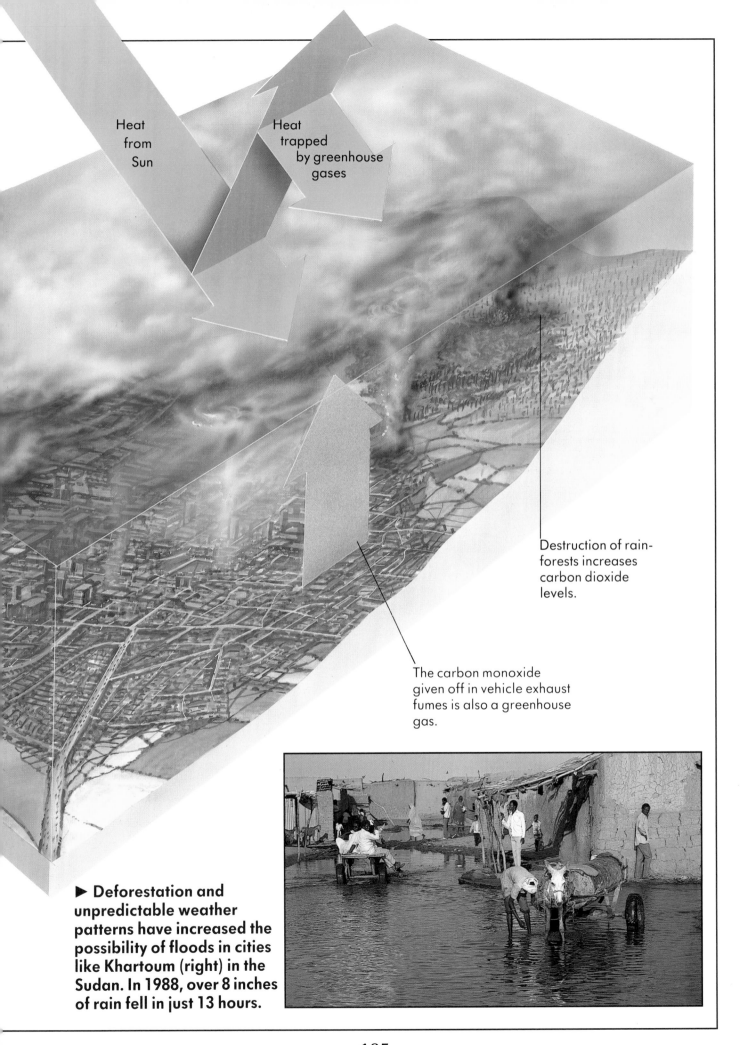

Heat
from
Sun

Heat
trapped
by greenhouse
gases

Destruction of rain-
forests increases
carbon dioxide
levels.

The carbon monoxide
given off in vehicle exhaust
fumes is also a greenhouse
gas.

▶ Deforestation and
unpredictable weather
patterns have increased the
possibility of floods in cities
like Khartoum (right) in the
Sudan. In 1988, over 8 inches
of rain fell in just 13 hours.

WHAT CAN WE DO?

Although floods can never be completely prevented, a variety of measures can be adopted to reduce their devastating impact. Improved warning and evacuation systems will ensure that fewer casualties occur. River levels are constantly monitored by the United States National Weather Service, which uses radar to predict the time, place, and amount of future rain and snow falls.

The Indian government is encouraging the replanting of trees in the Himalayas. This reforestation will provide people with firewood and will also keep enough trees growing to prevent the runoff of heavy rains. On a worldwide scale, slowing the rate of deforestation, and using alternative, cleaner sources of power, such as solar, wind, and wave power, can help to reduce carbon dioxide levels.

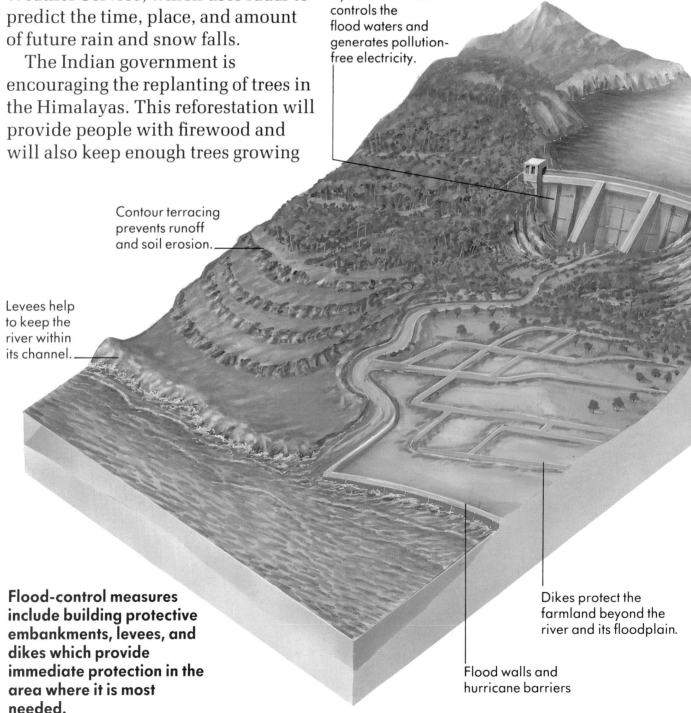

Hydroelectric dam controls the flood waters and generates pollution-free electricity.

Contour terracing prevents runoff and soil erosion.

Levees help to keep the river within its channel.

Flood-control measures include building protective embankments, levees, and dikes which provide immediate protection in the area where it is most needed.

Dikes protect the farmland beyond the river and its floodplain.

Flood walls and hurricane barriers

126

► Large-scale contour terracing of the steep hills on either side of a river traps rainwater in the soil and vegetation. Contour terracing, as seen in these rice terraces in the Philippines, also prevents soil erosion. When fertile topsoil is washed down into the river, it is deposited as silt on the river bed. This causes the height of the river bed to increase, making the river more prone to flooding.

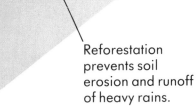

Reforestation prevents soil erosion and runoff of heavy rains.

Preventative measures
One method of flood prevention is to reinforce coastal defenses with huge slabs of concrete linked together. This is one of the systems used in Japan (shown right). For countries that are prone to flooding, special shelters can be built. Bangladesh has 63 such shelters. They are raised 13 feet above the ground. Over 350,000 people sought refuge in them from the flooding caused by the 1991 cyclone in that area.

FACTFILE: *Tidal Waves & Flooding*

The world's water

The total amount of water in the world's oceans is 840 million cubic miles. The Arctic and Antarctic ice sheets contain over 12 million cubic miles of water. Seventy percent of the world's freshwater supply is in a frozen state. Less than one percent of the world's total water supply is involved in the water cycle at any given time.

Tsunamis

Some *tsunamis* contain so much water that they flood more than ½ mile inland. Since 1819, over 100 *tsunamis* have reached the shores around Hawaii. A *tsunami* measuring 25 feet or more is recorded along the Japanese coastline every 15 years.

Flood control in China

The Chinese government is currently considering a plan to build a vast reservoir, over 375 miles long, to control the flood waters of the Yangtze River, the world's third largest river. The Yangtze produces a major flood on average every 10 years, and has claimed about 4 million lives in the twentieth century alone. The proposed reservoir will form part of the world's largest hydro-electric complex and will take about 18 years to build.

Floods in the future

Scientists have calculated that the amount of carbon dioxide in the atmosphere has increased by over 25 percent since 1850. If sea levels rise by 3¼ feet by the year 2030, as some scientists have predicted, 15 million Bangladeshis could be left homeless. Some of the world's cities which might also be at risk include London, Tokyo, Shanghai, Rome, and Rio de Janeiro.

Flood control in the USA

The U.S. government has spent more than $9 billion on flood control since the Flood Control Act in 1936. Along the Mississippi River, mattresses of concrete slabs have been laid along the riverbed and banks to prevent the river channel from becoming wider. In New Orleans, the Mississippi's natural defenses, its levees, have been reinforced with stone and concrete. They are over 23 feet high in places, and the river channel runs above the streets in some parts of the city. The floodplain of the Mississippi is one of the world's largest, reaching just over 125 miles wide at its widest point.

Recent floods
1990

Northern Europe – in February, storm winds of up to 100 mph caused huge sea waves and high tides. In The Netherlands, the tide reached its highest level for 37 years. In England, the Thames Barrier was raised.

South Korea – in September, South Korea experienced its heaviest rainfall for 83 years. The swollen Han River destroyed a 328-foot embankment in the capital city of Seoul, flooding residential and farming areas, leaving 137 dead or missing and 160,000 people homeless.

1991

Bangladesh – the worst cyclone in 20 years, with winds up to 143 mph, caused flooding over more than 310,000 square miles. With a death toll of over 250,000, an additional four million people risked death from starvation or disease.

China – in July the cities of Nanjing and Shanghai were threatened by the worst floods in 100 years as torrential rains caused the Yangtze River to rise above danger level. In two months, over 1,300 people died in floods that affected a total of 75 million people. One-quarter of the affected population was reported to be suffering from diseases like dysentery and typhoid.

Philippines – following a tropical storm, flash floods devastated the islands of Leyte, Samar, and Negros. In the town of Ormoc, some 342 miles from the capital Manila, over 2,000 people died. Many drowned in the streets in up to 10 feet of water. The floods affected a total of around 700,000 people. Government officials blamed the floods on the widespread deforestation being carried out in the area.

Chapter Six

FAMINE, DROUGHT AND PLAGUES

CONTENTS

INTRODUCTION

Long lines of starving people waiting patiently for food have become a familiar sight on our television screens and in our newspapers. Many developing countries are susceptible to droughts and other natural disasters, which force these people from their land and homes in search of food and water.

We can do little to control the natural disasters that occur in these parts of the world. Yet there is much that can be done to prevent such disasters from producing widespread famine.

WHAT IS FAMINE?

Famine is the long-term shortage of food. It can lead to hunger and malnutrition, which is a condition caused by a lack of food, or by a shortage of those foods needed to stay healthy. Later, disease and starvation follow, and eventually death.

Famine is a widespread problem that can strike in any corner of the developing world. It affects countries that are unable to provide enough food to feed their population. Famine has been responsible for the deaths of many millions of people, and affects many millions more at any one time. In 1991, the United Nations estimated that 32 million people in Africa alone were at risk from starvation.

The principal cause of famine is drought, which is the continuous lack of rainfall. Famine can also result from other natural disasters, such as hurricanes, earthquakes, and plagues of pests. In 1991, a cyclone caused severe flooding in Bangladesh. The resulting famine and disease threatened the lives of an estimated 4 million people.

Humans can themselves bring about famine, for example through wars. During the Nigerian civil war in 1967-70, soldiers prevented food supplies from reaching Biafra Province. As a result, around 1 million people starved to death.

▼ Crop failure is a major cause of famine. As the rains fail, soils become dry and dusty. Drought, poor farming practices and the removal of vegetation help to explain the appearance of the kind of landscape seen in Burkina Faso, in Africa (below).

▶ During a period of famine, millions of people are forced to leave their homes in search of food. Like this family in Ethiopia (right), many flock to special famine relief camps where food aid is distributed.

◀ The photograph (left) shows the dried-up bed of the River Niger, in Mali, during the dry season.

WHAT IS DROUGHT?

Drought is a long period with no rain or with much less rainfall than is normal for a particular area. Almost one-third of the land on Earth is prone to drought, which affects more than 600 million people.

During a drought, the soil becomes parched and cracked. The hard-baked surface cannot absorb any water, and so very little moisture is retained in the soil. The dry and dusty topsoil is worn away by wind and rain, leaving behind patches of barren land.

Drought is a natural disaster that can affect any country in the world. However, its effects are made much worse in the developing world by a number of factors. They include overpopulation, overgrazing, and cutting down trees to provide firewood.

Hot, dry winds and very high temperatures, combined with a lack of rainfall and the evaporation of moisture in the ground, produce the conditions of drought. In some areas, periods of drought alternate with periods of flood, continually destroying food crops and farmland.

Hot, dry winds

Eroded topsoil

Dried-up wells

Failed crops

◀ Thousands of people are forced to stand in line for food after the failure of their crops through drought.

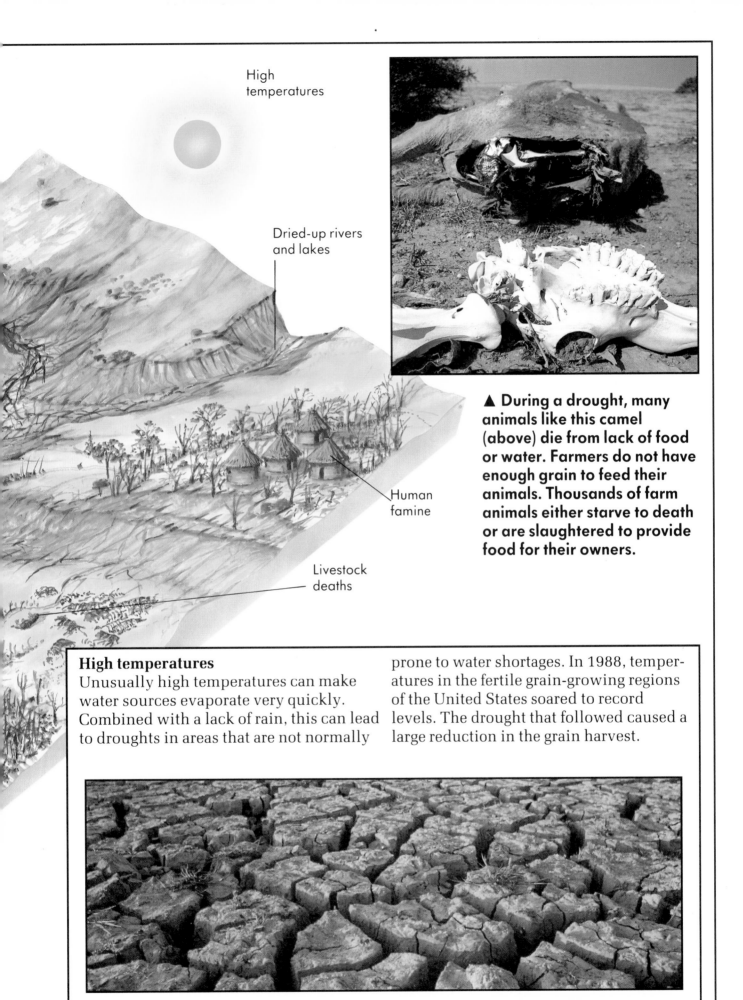

High
temperatures

Dried-up rivers
and lakes

Human
famine

Livestock
deaths

▲ During a drought, many animals like this camel (above) die from lack of food or water. Farmers do not have enough grain to feed their animals. Thousands of farm animals either starve to death or are slaughtered to provide food for their owners.

High temperatures

Unusually high temperatures can make water sources evaporate very quickly. Combined with a lack of rain, this can lead to droughts in areas that are not normally prone to water shortages. In 1988, temperatures in the fertile grain-growing regions of the United States soared to record levels. The drought that followed caused a large reduction in the grain harvest.

WHY DO DROUGHTS HAPPEN?

Droughts are frequently caused by natural factors, such as changes in weather patterns.

In 1982-83 the weather system in many parts of the world was dramatically altered by a phenomenon called "El Niño." El Niño was responsible for extreme weather conditions, including dust storms in Australia and drought in Southeast Asia.

Yet drought can also result from, or be made worse by, human activities. Trees help to keep soil fertile and to store water. When they are removed, the soil can no longer retain water. It becomes dry and dusty, and soil erosion sets in. As the land is deforested and overgrazed, it turns to desert. This spreading of desert areas is called desertification.

As warm moist air rises up from the oceans, it cools. Water vapor in the air condenses and turns back into water droplets, which fall as rain or snow. This process is called the water cycle.

Very high temperatures cause rain to evaporate as it reaches the warm ground. When air travels to the sheltered, or leeward, side of a mountain, it sinks down and heats up. Evaporation makes the rain clouds disappear, creating a rain shadow zone where little or no rain falls.

Water droplets evaporate and rain clouds disappear (rain shadow zone)

Dry air heats up as it sinks

◄ Each year, many thousands of trees are burned to clear land for cash crops, which supply poorer countries with badly needed foreign currency.

Water vapor condenses and forms clouds.

Warm, moist air rises and cools.

Rain and snow fall

▼ Hot, dry weather conditions in western Europe in 1976 caused widespread drought. Although its effects were serious, particularly for farmers, the drought did not result in famine.

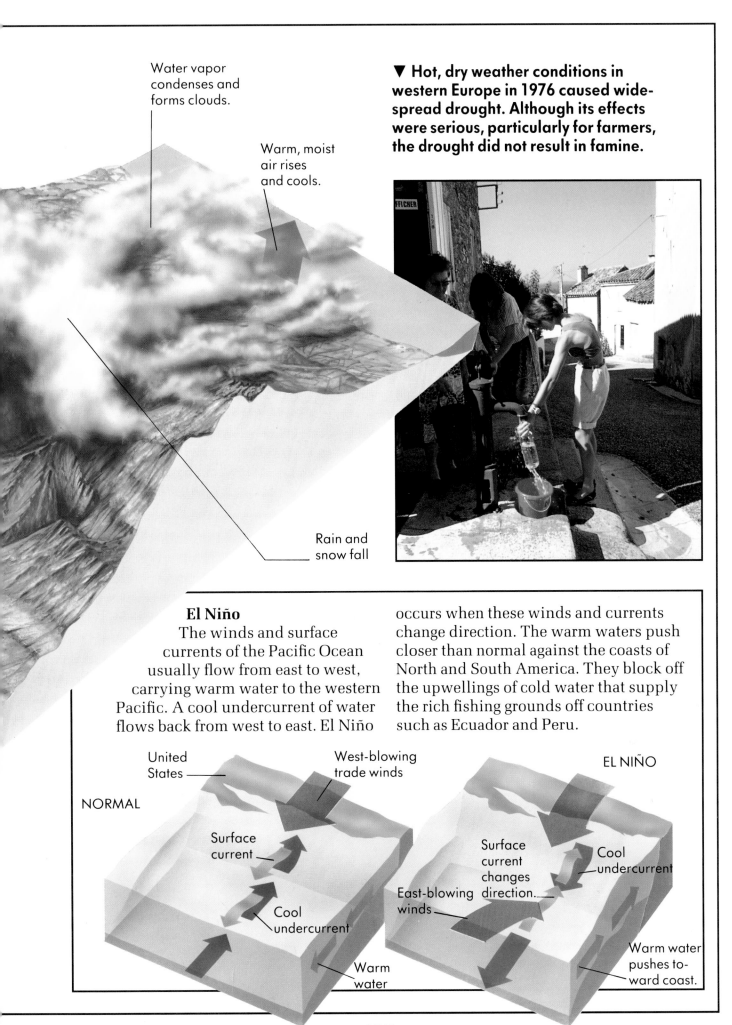

El Niño

The winds and surface currents of the Pacific Ocean usually flow from east to west, carrying warm water to the western Pacific. A cool undercurrent of water flows back from west to east. El Niño occurs when these winds and currents change direction. The warm waters push closer than normal against the coasts of North and South America. They block off the upwellings of cold water that supply the rich fishing grounds off countries such as Ecuador and Peru.

NORMAL

United States

West-blowing trade winds

Surface current

Cool undercurrent

Warm water

EL NIÑO

Surface current changes direction.

East-blowing winds

Cool undercurrent

Warm water pushes toward coast.

137

THE DAMAGE

In a drought-ravaged land, there are no supplies of food and water for the people, no water to make the crops grow, and no fodder to feed the animals. Hungry and weak, people are forced to abandon their land in search of food and water. Some travel hundreds of miles to food camps, or to the cities. In Nouakchott, Mauritania, over half of the population of 350,000 are refugees from the surrounding countryside.

In India, disaster can follow the failure or late arrival of the monsoon rains. When the rains failed in 1987, some 15 million Indian farmers had no work. About 192 million people across Asia were affected by drought.

The map below shows which areas of the world are affected by drought. It strikes mainly at the continents of Africa and Asia. Drought has been relentless in many African countries since the 1960s. Central and South America have also suffered periods of drought.

◀ Dust storms, such as the one in Mali, left, are a regular feature of drought. High winds blow the dry topsoil into thick clouds of dusty, swirling particles. These storms can be so thick that they shut out the sunlight and make daytime look like night.

► These people in northern Kenya are digging for water in a dried-up river bed. As water supplies run out, the only water left to drink is often contaminated. Dirty drinking water can lead to outbreaks of diseases such as cholera and typhoid.

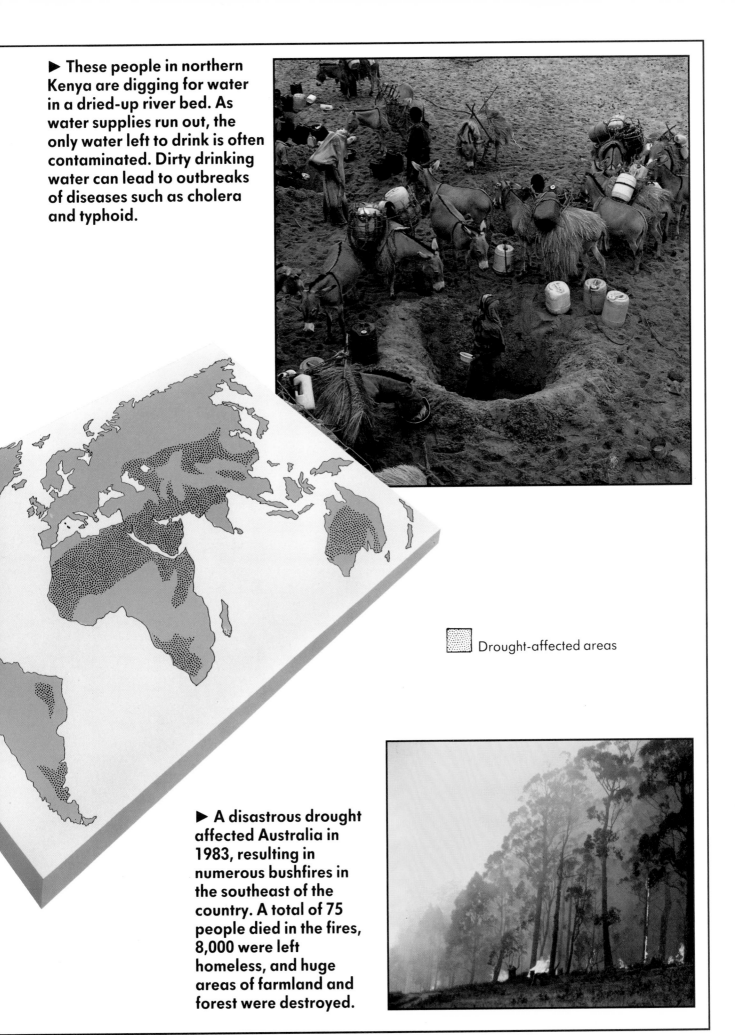

Drought-affected areas

► A disastrous drought affected Australia in 1983, resulting in numerous bushfires in the southeast of the country. A total of 75 people died in the fires, 8,000 were left homeless, and huge areas of farmland and forest were destroyed.

WHAT ARE PLAGUES?

A plague is an invasion by large numbers of animals or insects. The animals often carry disease, and they eat enormous quantities of growing crops and stored grain. This can bring about a severe famine.

Some of the most destructive plagues consist of swarms of locusts. A single swarm may contain up to 50 billion insects.

Plagues of locusts have threatened several African countries in recent years. Rains in 1988 helped to relieve the drought. However, when combined with warmer weather, they provided ideal conditions for the locusts to breed. As a result, swarms of migratory locusts swept across North and Central Africa, destroying the much-needed harvest there.

Locusts

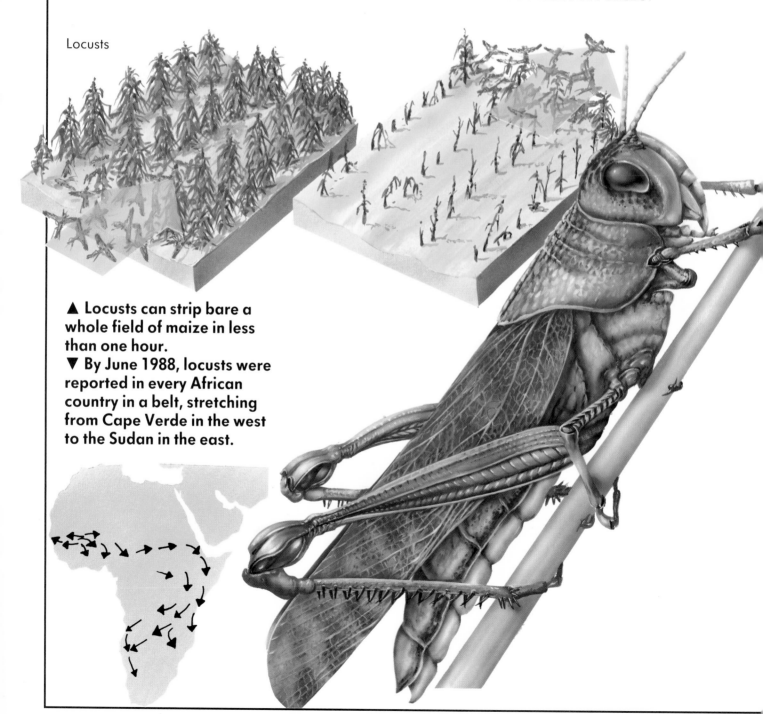

▲ Locusts can strip bare a whole field of maize in less than one hour.
▼ By June 1988, locusts were reported in every African country in a belt, stretching from Cape Verde in the west to the Sudan in the east.

► Locusts fly thousands of miles in search of food. Locust invasions, such as the one in Dakar, Senegal, shown right, have plagued farmers throughout the world since ancient times. Locusts will eat any kind of vegetation, and can consume more than their own body weight of food in just one day.

▼◄ A locust is a type of adult grasshopper with wings. Its body is about 3 inches long. The female locust can produce hundreds of eggs in a single breeding season. As locusts become crowded and restless, they begin to migrate in swarms to other areas. The swarms can be so large, they block out the sunlight.

Kangaroos

Animal plagues can also involve large mammals such as kangaroos and goats. More than 3 million kangaroos are killed in Australia each year. Australian farmers consider that some of the 50 different kinds of kangaroo are pests. They feed and drink in the same areas as the farmers' sheep and cattle.

Controlling the kangaroo population has proved difficult as they cannot easily be contained by fencing.

FAMINE STRIKES

The effects of famine are often felt long after a disaster such as drought has passed. Many people, especially children and the elderly, become very weak from hunger and malnutrition. They begin to suffer from diarrhea and other famine-related diseases, such as kwashiorkor and marasmus. Their faces and stomachs swell up, and their legs and arms are frail and stick-like.

The threat of continuing famine is made worse when farmers fail to plant the following year's harvest. This happens either because all the seed has been eaten to avoid further starvation, or because the people are too weak to work on their land. Many may also have left their farms in search of food elsewhere.

▼ **Short-term solutions to famine include the distribution of millions of tons of food aid to people in huge famine relief camps.**

▶ Aid workers involved in the supply and distribution of food aid encounter many problems. Only foods such as grains and milk powder are suitable for famine relief operations because fresh foods will rot. A lack of roads and vehicles, as well as the problems of civil war and fighting, are just some of the other obstacles. The aid worker shown right is distributing ration cards to people in line for food.

Famine areas

The developing nations that are ravaged by famine are also among the world's poorest. One of the worst droughts in memory is now hitting southern Africa. Crops are dying and grazing lands are baked dry.

The problems of drought are made worse by the agricultural methods in these countries, which do not provide enough food to feed the population. There is no money to import food supplies from countries that have spare grain to sell.

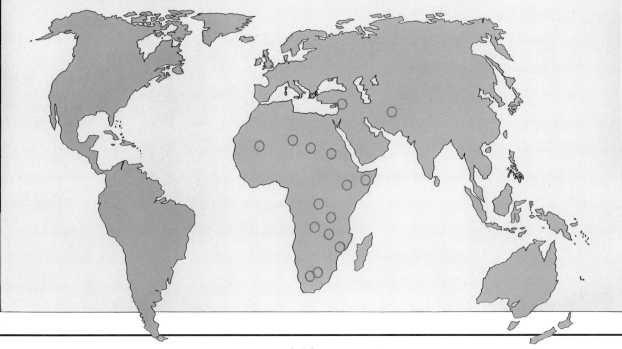

PAST DISASTERS

Like present-day disasters, famines, droughts, and plagues in the past have been due to various causes. Rats brought plague to the Indian city of Bombay in 1898, killing around 12.5 million people. Flooding by the Yangtze River was responsible for the deaths from famine of more than 3 million Chinese in 1931.

Records of drought disasters in ancient times tell of famine in Egypt. When the annual flooding of the Nile River failed, the fertile farmlands were deprived of vital water supplies. Scientists have even discovered evidence of a drought that occurred in the United States more than 2,000 years ago, by examining the annual growth rings in the wood of old trees.

The first recorded plague occurred in Athens in the 1st century B.C. A plague in the city of Rome in A.D. 262 led to the death of 5,000 people a day. Biblical references in the Book of Exodus describe Egypt after a plague of locusts 3,500 years ago.

▼ A severe famine hit Ireland between 1841 and 1851 after disease destroyed the potato crop. The population was reduced by about 2.5 million through starvation and emigration. The picture below shows starving peasants begging for food outside a workhouse.

The Black Death

The plague known as the Black Death could be recognized by the black spots and swellings that appeared on people's bodies. It was a kind of bubonic plague, which is an epidemic disease passed to humans by rats. Between 1347 and 1351, the Black Death killed an estimated 25 million people throughout Asia and Europe, making it the greatest plague recorded in history.

The plague was brought to Europe by rats on board the spice ships that arrived from the East. Rats (below) are among the world's most destructive creatures. Each year, they consume vast amounts of the world's food crops.

FIGHTING DROUGHT

One of the principal aims in the fight against drought is to store as much water as possible during periods of rain. In Burkina Faso, curved lines of stones around fields prevent the run-off of rainwater and reduce soil erosion. Elsewhere, small dams made of soil help to retain the rainwater.

Slowing down the rate of deforestation is another important anti-drought measure. Trees soak in moisture like a sponge, releasing it slowly. They also add moisture to the air, as water passes out through their leaves in a process called transpiration.

To prevent the spread of the desert, sand dunes are anchored with brushwood fences and lines of fast-growing trees, like eucalyptus. The sand dunes around Nouakchott in Mauritania have been held down with branches, which also act as a windbreak.

In poorer countries solutions to combat drought include hillside terracing and the planting of trees such as acacia, which can tap water sources deep underground.

In Mexico, steep slopes have been planted with spineless cacti. The plants conserve the topsoil and provide food for animals during the dry season.

Trees act as windbreaks and stabilize sand dunes.

Water for irrigation can be pumped up from aquifers deep below the surface.

◀ **Without the water from irrigation, these crops on the Ganges Plain of India (left) would die.**

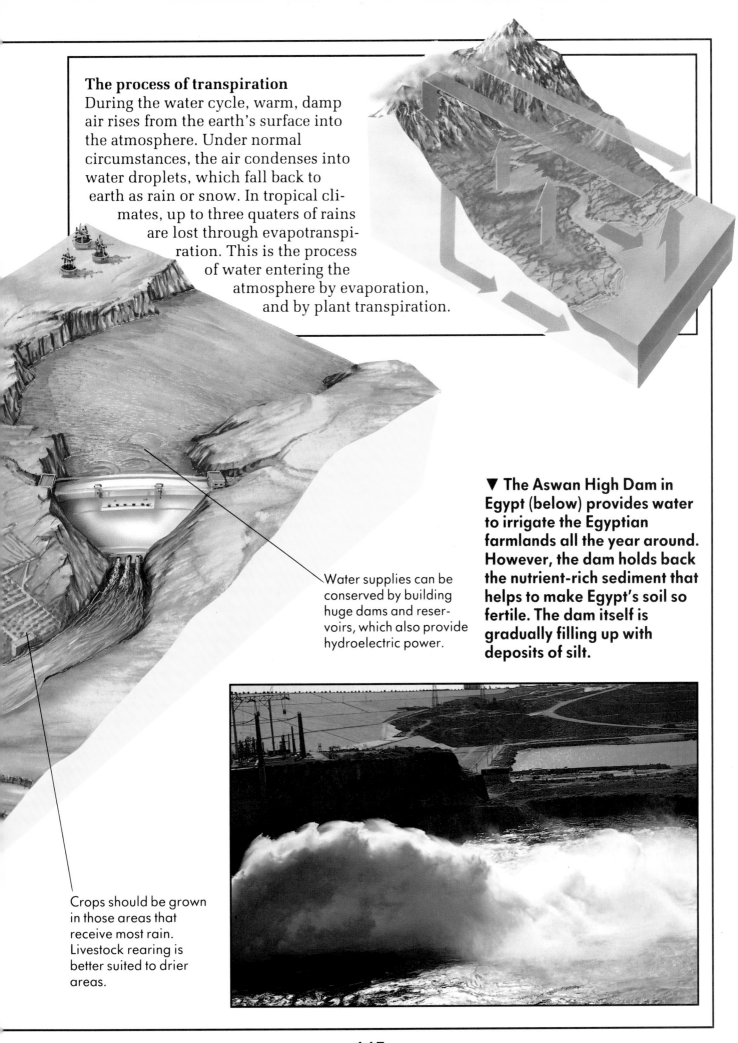

The process of transpiration
During the water cycle, warm, damp air rises from the earth's surface into the atmosphere. Under normal circumstances, the air condenses into water droplets, which fall back to earth as rain or snow. In tropical climates, up to three quaters of rains are lost through evapotranspiration. This is the process of water entering the atmosphere by evaporation, and by plant transpiration.

Water supplies can be conserved by building huge dams and reservoirs, which also provide hydroelectric power.

▼ The Aswan High Dam in Egypt (below) provides water to irrigate the Egyptian farmlands all the year around. However, the dam holds back the nutrient-rich sediment that helps to make Egypt's soil so fertile. The dam itself is gradually filling up with deposits of silt.

Crops should be grown in those areas that receive most rain. Livestock rearing is better suited to drier areas.

FAMINE AID

Without the aid efforts of international organisations working in famine-stricken countries in the 1970s and 1980s, the numbers of people dying from starvation and disease would have been even greater. In 1991, the United Nations World Food Program estimated that up to 20 million people depended on emergency food aid.

In the short term, famine aid involves bringing food supplies to affected areas to prevent people from starving to death. Inadequate transportation, poor roads, and war or tribal fighting are some of the barriers to the distribution of food aid.

In the long term, however, international aid must involve helping the economic development of poor countries so that they can increase their foreign earnings. These countries could then purchase equipment and technology from abroad, and also finance their own water management and other antidrought programs.

Machinery and farm equipment are donated by richer countries.

New deep wells are built.

Aid agencies provide the victims of famine with education and training, as well as with food and medical aid. Local farmers are encouraged to adopt improved farming methods. These include irrigation, contour plowing and growing more resistant crop varieties.

Relief trucks bring food supplies.

Cereals and other basic foods are distributed in the refugee camps.

Immunization prevents the spread of disease.

Aid workers encourage self-help among the local population

► In 1992, over 1.25 million tons of overseas food aid will be needed in Ethiopia to avoid the deaths of 7 million famine victims. Trucks and fuel supplies are also needed to ensure that the food aid reaches the famine areas.

Food storage and processing facilities need to be improved to reduce the huge quantities of grain lost after each harvest. More than 70 million tons of key cereals, such as rice and corn, are lost every year.

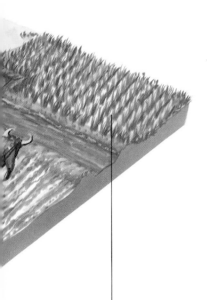

Improved farming methods are introduced.

Planning ahead
In the picture below, millet seed is being distributed to the villagers of Tchawai village, near Bokoro, in Chad.

Economic policies for the future must concentrate on producing more food crops for the country's own population, rather than cash crops.

WHAT CAN WE DO?

Although droughts and famines cannot be completely wiped out, certain measures can be taken to reduce their impact.

The production of traditional crops, such as yams, sweet potato, and cassava, is being increased. A new bread has already been developed, which is made from cassava or sorghum flour instead of wheat flour. New farming methods and crops can encourage people to find their own solutions to the drought problem, without having to leave their land.

Modern technology helps to control pests such as locusts, which breed in huge numbers in warm, damp conditions. When satellite pictures show significant rises in the moisture levels of their breeding grounds, these areas are sprayed with pesticides. Scientists have also used computers to establish a link between ocean temperatures and drought. With this method, they predicted accurately the recent droughts in the Sahel and in northeastern Brazil.

Since the 1970s, aid agencies and numerous charities in the developed world have raised millions of dollars to fund their aid programs. The money has come as a result of frequent advertising campaigns, appeals for money, and huge fund-raising efforts. Their work has helped to increase our awareness of the suffering of famine victims and of the problems they face.

▶ In Ethiopia, the government has organized thousands of farmers to build dams and dig terraces that help to retain rainwater. In the photo, right, trees are being planted to protect newly created earth dams, called diguettes.

◀▼ Education and training, such as this practical mechanics course shown left in Dakar, Senegal, are important aspects of any program to aid economic development.

Population growth

In many developing countries, the rate of population growth is so rapid that there are too many mouths to feed. In Bangladesh, one of the world's most densely populated and poorest countries, about 7 babies are born every minute.

Controlling the growth of the population is a key issue in the fight against hunger and famine. These women in Calcutta, India (below), are learning about a government campaign to reduce the number of babies born each year.

FACTFILE: *Famine, Drought & Plagues*

Population growth
About 90 percent of the world's population growth occurs in the developing world. The world's population is increasing by 80 million each year. By the year 2070, the population of the world will have reached 10 billion people.

United Nations
The World Food Program (WFP) of the United Nations gives priority aid to poor countries with food shortages. It has recently funded projects to stop desertification in Burkina Faso, to undertake water supply and reforestation work in India, and to conserve soil and water in Haiti.

A plague of birds
Millions of red-billed queleas, which are tiny sparrowlike birds, fly across Africa each year. They swoop down on the ripening crops, consuming thousands of tons of rice, millet, and wheat.

Agriculture in India
In 1978, drought affected two-thirds of India, when less than 60 percent of the expected rainfall fell in the worst-hit areas. A famine disaster was avoided because of new farming techniques introduced during the 1950s and 1960s. During this so-called "green revolution" in Indian agriculture, irrigation became more widespread.

Also, new types of wheat and rice that produced higher yields were grown. Stockpiles of food surpluses averted the threat of famine.

Recent disasters
1990
Spain – the most severe drought since 1945 affected parts of Spain. Irrigation was banned in the southwest of the country, and water rationing was introduced in the Basque region in the northeast.

Jordan – emergency food relief was needed for almost half a million refugees who had fled from Kuwait and Iraq following the Iraqi invasion of Kuwait.

Ethiopia – government and opposition soldiers agreed to open up the Red Sea port of Massawa to let in U.N. ships carrying relief supplies. Food aid was needed for the 4 million people starving in the provinces of Tigre and Wollo.

1991
Africa – the famine situation was judged to be critical in Angola, Ethiopia, Mozambique, Somalia, and Sudan. In all these countries, the problems of food distribution were made worse by civil war.

1992
Mozambique – drought in six of the country's provinces led to serious grain shortages. The civil war prevented the cultivation of food crops and the adequate distribution of food supplies. One million refugees fled into neighboring Malawi, where harvests were also badly affected by drought.

Botswana – with only one-fifth of the normal crop area planted this year, grain will be in short supply and food prices will rise. In a country where an estimated 1 in every 4 children suffers from malnutrition, large quantities of cereals will have to be imported to avert famine disaster.

Somalia – on January 12, the water supply in the capital, Mogadishu, was cut off, and thousands of tons of food aid in the city's port were looted. Hundreds of thousands of refugees in nearby camps were on the brink of starvation. Around 700 Somali refugees a day were flocking into neighboring Kenya. Fighting between rival groups has continued in the capital since November 1991.

Deforestation
In the Indian state of Maharastra, deforestation is blamed for drying up the water supplies in a total of 23,000 villages. Deforestation in the Ethiopian Highlands has reduced the amount of water flowing into the Nile River. This has disastrous consequences for the many farmers who use the river's water to irrigate their farmlands.

GLOSSARY

acid rain – rain which has acid in it formed as a result of pollution.

aftershocks – extra movements of the ground that occur after the first shock waves.

air pressure – the weight of the air in the lower layers of the atmosphere pressing down on the earth.

aquifer – an underground reservoir of water. It is formed out of porous rocks, such as sandstone, that hold water.

archeologist – someone who pieces together history from evidence such as the ruins of buildings, statues, pottery, and wall paintings.

atmosphere – the envelope of gases that surround the Earth. The atmosphere protects us from the sun and also provides us with the oxygen we need to breathe.

avalanche – the downward movement of a mass of ice and snow.

basalt – a type of rock formed from dark, runny lava.

bubonic plague – a disease that causes swellings under the skin. It is passed to humans by rats and other small animals.

caldera – a huge round crater formed when a volcano collapses, or when the top blows off during an eruption.

carbon dioxide – one of the gases found naturally in the atmosphere. It is also produced by burning fossil fuels.

cash crop – a crop that is grown to be sold, and not to provide food for local people.

channel – the sides and bottom of a river inside which water normally flows.

condense – to turn from water vapor into tiny drops of water.

core – the central part of the earth, which is made up mainly of iron. The inner core is thought to be solid and the outer core is liquid and very hot.

creep – the slow, almost unnoticeable, movement of loose soil down the surface of a slope.

crust – the thin outer layer of rock around the Earth.

cyclone – the name for tropical storms when they occur in the Indian Ocean.

debris – loose solid material such as soil, mud, small pieces of rock, and stones.

delta – a fan shaped area of land which is formed when a river deposits large amounts of silt at its mouth. The river divides into separate channels as it flows to the sea.

developing country – a poor country that is trying to improve its economy and give its people a better way of life.

dike – a protective wall, usually built of earth reinforced with stone, which keeps water away from farmland.

drought – a long period of dryness with a continuous lack of rainfall, or with less rainfall than usual.

Dust Bowl – an area of the Great Plains that suffered a severe drought in the 1930s.

dust storm – swirling clouds of fine sand, dust, and topsoil that are blown off the land.

earthquake – a movement or tremor of the earth's crust, often caused by plates moving against each other.

earth tremor – the violent trembling of the ground that occurs during and after an earthquake.

El Niño – a reversal in the direction of winds and ocean currents that causes dramatic changes in the world's weather. It is named after the Spanish word for "Christ child."

embankment – a wall built along the banks of a river to prevent it from flooding.

epicenter – the place on the earth's surface directly above the focus of the earthquake.

erosion – the removal or gradual destruction of a surface by the action of water, ice, or wind. Human activities such as tree-felling, as well as natural weathering can also lead to erosion.

eruption – the violent release of steam, rocks, dust, and ash through an opening in the earth's surface.

evacuate – to remove people from a place that is considered to be dangerous.

evaporate – when a liquid is heated and turns into a vapor.

evolution – the way in which animals and plants slowly change over millions of years to adapt to changes in the climate or the environment, or to protect themselves from predators.

eye – the calm, nearly cloudless center of a hurricane, cyclone, or typhoon.

famine – a long term shortage of food supplies.

fertile – suitable for growing healthy crops.

flash flood – a sudden torrent of water that sweeps over dry land. It is usually caused by a heavy rainstorm.

fault – a weak point inside the earth's crust where the rock layers have ruptured and slipped.

floodplain – the land on either side of a river that is covered with water when the river overflows its banks.

focus – the point inside the earth's crust where the shock waves of an earthquake are released.

food aid – the supply and distribution of food to famine victims.

front – the boundary between a mass of warm, moist air and a mass of cold, dry air.

geologist – someone who studies the layers of rock in the earth's crust.

geothermal – heat from inside the earth.

global warming – an increase in the earth's temperature due to a buildup of greenhouse gases, such as carbon dioxide, in the atmosphere.

gravity – a force that pulls one object toward another. The earth's gravity pulls on all solids, liquids, and gases.

greenhouse gas – one of the gases in the atmosphere that traps heat from the sun and keeps the earth warm.

groundwater – water that is found in rocks and soil beneath the surface.

hemisphere – half a sphere. The equator divides the earth into the northern hemisphere and the southern hemisphere.

hurricane – a spinning tropical storm that occurs over the Atlantic Ocean.

hydrologist – a scientist who studies the movement of water on, below, and above the earth's surface.

igneous rock – rock formed from hardened lava or magma.

impermeable rock – rock which water cannot seep through, such as granite.

irrigation – the artificial watering of crops in dry areas.

lahar – a mixture of rocks, snow and ice, and the ash from an erupting volcano.

landslide – the downhill movement of large amounts of rock and soil.

lava – magma which reaches the surface and pours out of a volcano.

levee – a bank beside a river that prevents the river's water from spilling onto the land.

Lithosphere – the outer solid layer which surrounds the earth. It consists of the crust and the upper mantle.

L (long) wave – a type of shock wave which travels along the surface during an earthquake and causes the most serious damage.

lubricate – to make a surface slippery.

magma – the hot liquid rock beneath the earth's crust.

malnutrition – a condition caused by a lack or shortage of healthy food.

mantle – the layer of rock that lies between the outer crust and the core of the earth. The upper mantle is in a semiliquid state.

Mercalli scale – a system used to measure the strength of an earthquake according to the amount of damage caused and the effects felt at the time of the tremors.

meteorologist – someone who studies information about weather conditions and prepares a weather forecast.

monsoon – a warm wind that brings heavy summer rains to parts of Asia.

mudflow – the rapid downhill movement of soil mixed with water.

nutrients - nourishing ingredients.

oceanic ridge – a type of plate boundary where new ocean floor is created by rising magma, which cools and hardens.

overgrazing – the effect when too many animals graze on grasslands and destroy the vegetation.

overpopulation – when too many people live in a country that cannot produce enough food to feed them.

pesticide – a chemical that is sprayed onto crops or land to destroy certain pests.

plague – an invasion by large numbers of animals. "Plague" also means an epidemic disease that kills large numbers of a population.

plate – one of the huge sections which make up the earth's crust. The plates are continuously moving.

plate boundary – the place where two or more plates in the earth's crust meet. Most earthquakes occur along plate boundaries.

polder – a low-lying area where the water has been drained away and the land reclaimed.

pollute – to poison the air or water by allowing a buildup of substances such as waste gases.

porous rock – rock with tiny holes in it, like a sponge, which water can seep though.

P (primary) wave – a type of shock wave which is released from the focus of an earthquake. P waves are the fastest type of seismic wave.

pumice – a light volcanic rock formed from lava. Pumice is very light due to the gas bubbles which are trapped in it and can float on water.

reforestation – large-scale replanting of trees in an area which has been deforested.

Richter scale – a system that measures the strength of an earthquake by using information recorded by a seismograph.

sandstone – a coarse rock made up of grains of sand joined together.

satellite – a small object moving around a larger one, such as the moon moving around the earth.

saturated – filled with the maximum amount of a liquid or solid substance.

scarp – the steep slope left behind when a landslide falls away.

secondary tremor – violent trembling of the earth's surface which is caused by surface, or L waves and results in the most serious earthquake damage.

sediment – a mixture of rocks and soil that is carried along by a river.

seismic wave (shock wave) – a huge burst of energy which is released from the rocks inside the earth during an earthquake.

seismograph – an instrument which measures and studies shock waves to find out more about earthquakes.

seismologist – a scientist who measures and studies shock waves to find out more about earthquakes.

shale – a kind of soft rock made from tiny pieces of mud and clay.

shock wave – a wave of energy that is released from the center of an earthquake.

silica – a mineral in the earth's crust.

slab avalanche – the downward movement of a large chunk of solid snow.

slump – the movement down a slope of a block of rock and soil. The slumped block tilts back towards the slope.

soil erosion – the process of topsoil being removed due to weathering usually by wind and rain.

storm surge – massive waves which build up far out at sea as a tropical storm blows in.

subduction zone – a type of plate boundary where part of the earth's crust is destroyed as one plate is forced down beneath another.

S (secondary) wave – a type of shock wave that travels from the focus of the earthquake up to the surface.

temperate – describes a climate which has four seasons.

thermal current – a current of air that is rising because it has been heated.

transform fault – a type of plate boundary where two plates move against one another. Transform faults occur at right angles to oceanic ridges.

tremor – a violent shaking of the ground caused by an earthquake's shock waves.

transpiration – the process of plants giving off water vapor through their leaves.

tropics – the part of the earth between the tropic of Cancer and the tropic of Capricorn. The weather is hottest at the equator.

tsunami – a series of huge sea waves caused by shock waves from an earthquake or volcano.

tuff – ash which has been ejected from an erupting volcano and hardens into volcanic rock.

typhoon – the name for tropical storms when they occur in the Far East.

unstable – describes a slope that is likely to start moving downward.

vent – the hole in the top of a volcano through which the molten magma is forced out.

volcano – an opening in the earth's surface through which hot rocks and gases can escape.

water cycle – the continuous movement of water from the oceans, up through the air to the clouds, and back down to earth as either rain or snow.

wet-snow avalanche – the downhill sliding movement of large chunks of wet snow.

INDEX

With special thanks to the following photo libraries:

Allan Cash Photo Library, Ancient Art and Architecture Collection, Bruce Coleman Limited, Charles de Vere, Environmental Picture Library, Earthquake Research Institute of the University of Tokyo, Eye Ubiquitous, Frank Lane Picture Agency, Frank Spooner Pictures, Geoscience Features, The Hulton Picture Company, The Hutchinson Library, Mary Evans Picture Library, Natural History Photographic Agency, Paul Galvin, Panos Pictures, Planet Earth Pictures, Popperfoto, Robert Harding Picture Library, Roger Vlitos, Spectrum Color Library, Science Photo Library, Topham Picture Source.